Between the Posts

155 powerful practical suggestions,
techniques and key questions, that will
enable you to supercharge your goals, move
forward and unlock the confidence you
need to innovate, influence and...
...turn passion into profit!

A personal reminder.

An almighty almanac of
blogposts and articles.

Principles that I speak,
train and write about.

ENJOY!

www.michaeldavidpatterson.com

Between the Posts

...is dedicated to NO ONE PERSON, but to all those committed, devoted, enthusiastic, passionate and single-minded individuals that set the example, that strive every day to make a difference - to simply, become better!

People whose stories have inspired me to be a finer businessman, husband and father.

Penalty Takers: *Fulfill Potential, Exceed Expectations, Are Visionaries, People of Integrity. They Create Magic, Deliver and are Trustworthy.*

They step up to the spot and 'Inspire Others'.

"I hope like me, you'll find this book rich with strategies for working, living and loving better than we currently do."

Michael

www.michaeldavidpatterson.com

ISBN: 978-1-326-17526-9

Previous books by Michael Patterson -

Time For Kick-Off:
Succeeding in Business and in Life
When the Whistle Blows!

It's a Brand New

Game: How Barcelona, Beckham
and Big Business, have transformed
soccer in the 21st century!

Victus:
Building an Appetite to Take On the
World!

The Gulliver
Principle:
Opportunities lie in all directions.

Contents

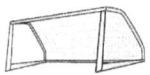 **PRE-Match team-talk:**

We all from time to time have great thoughts, ideas and suggestions we'd love to see implemented. We may even write them down, express them vocally to others and more than likely share them with friends. These days via all forms of social media - inspirational updates, blogs and tweets are dispatched instantly throughout the globe.

In the meantime - Do you follow up on your thoughts, take heed of your own counsel, stay true to the course of action you have outlined in your shared comments.

Encouragement - As not to lose sight of the desired aims and ambitions each of us may have currently in our lives, this book is a gentle reminder of a selection of my blog posts in recent years. An exciting opportunity to act upon what has been said 'Between The Posts', that we may continue to strive to find success, follow the dream and achieve our ultimate GOAL!

1. A Slice of Significance...

In 1960 Thomas Monaghan and his brother, James, bought a tiny pizza joint named DomiNicks for $500. By the mid-1990s, Domino's was a worldwide brand, and Thomas Monaghan was one of the wealthiest men alive. In 2010, he joined The Giving Pledge, a charity drive by Bill Gates and Warren Buffett to inspire American billionaires to give away the majority of their wealth.

Monaghan is a role model on how to transition from success to significance.

2. Turn the Ordinary into the Extraordinary...

Fred Shea was the United States postal

worker in author Mark Sanborn's 2004 book The Fred Factor. He always went the extra mile, was exceptional in his role, and exceeded expectations at every turn.

Have you become a FRED yet?

3. Don't Leave it to Others...

As the young three year old girl knelt at her bedside, she began to offer a prayer in which she just recited the alphabet - "A,B,C,D", when her mother interrupted her and asked her what she was doing. She simply stated,"I just couldn't think of what to say tonight, but he knows what I wanted to say - so I gave God all the letters and he will put them into the right order."

How often do we do that with others? We respect, value and trust our family, friends and work colleagues, and that's great. However, often our communication is unclear and we

*leave it to them to figure out, to put our
instructions in order and prioritize. Then we
become disappointed when things are not done
the way we CLEARLY explained them!*

4. Be Prepared...

Maybe not as boy scouts,
but within football – the
scouting network is
invaluable. These scouts
play an important role in discovering and
unearthing hidden gems, the stars of the
future.

*How well do you help prepare, enhance
and develop those that will lead tomorrow?*

5. The Magic Sponge...

Many years ago, our coach
was a full time window
cleaner. Whenever a player
went down injured,
suffered cuts and was bleeding profusely,
on came coach with his trusty sponge. We

as players were sure it was filled with the same water he had used all week on his route. It was indeed a MAGIC sponge, because when we saw him coming towards us....every player made a miraculous recovery.

Times are different - advancing technology, workplace etiquette and increased standards allow us now to Step Forward, Embrace Change & Reap the Rewards!

6. Making Every Touch Count...

Adidas have a range of boot: The Lethal Zone. Pass, Dribble, Sweet Spot, Drive and First Touch are the 5 lethal zones.

Within your business are you fully aware of your lethal zones? What makes you different, stand out from the rest. Do you offer a truly exceptional customer experience worth telling others about?

7. Becoming Invaluable...

Gareth Bale was discovered as an eight year old, playing in a six-a-side tournament one August Bank holiday. Beginning his career as a left back, gradually over the years his position and role in the team changed. He became more influential, scored more goals and became more valuable than ever before!
In the summer of 2013 and at nearly 100 million Euros, he reportedly became the most expensive player in footballing history!

Could a change of role make you more of an asset, more effective and allow you to fulfill your unlimited potential?

8. Lego of the Past...

Your playing style now has to surprise,

inspire and delight. You have the ability to change the pace and shape of a game and effectively contribute right from the off. Your role is now to raise expectations and exceed them.

To achieve winning results as part of a fascinating and innovative team of players, penalty takers every one.

 *Skills, talents & abilities: Think transferable - otherwise, that is what you'll become!*

9. Way More Than Just Taking to the Field...

You are probably fine with that part. Clean strip and gentle warm up, whilst the sun beams brightly. Looking out toward the adoring fans that have paid hard earned money for your product. Often in squads, we identify players who believe that their role is to turn up as expected and then wait for instructions.

In the Premiership of business, we are way beyond that now. Showing up and making a couple of predictable passes is no longer acceptable.

10. Rewarding Poor Behaviour...

We can make and take many courageous decisions throughout our careers, enjoy much success on many levels. We can help our businesses to record growth and profits, innovate, create jobs and inspire those around us.

Yet more often than not, we can be remembered for the one poor choice that we made - thus tarnishing our formidable legacy. (i.e. The Zinedine Zidane head butt against Marco Materazzi in the 2006 World Cup Final)

11. Inspiring Siblings...

To a lady who was filled with courage, strength and compassion, who lived a life of service to others. A devoted wife and mother to her husband and family.
Janet Ewing (06/08/53 - 10/01/07).
My inspirational sister who taught me much through how she lived her life. Who always believed in her 'baby' brother and who continually created so many opportunities for others.

Believe in others and help them believe in themselves!

12. Honey Thaljieh...

As a peace ambassador and captain of the Palestinian national team, Honey broke down barriers and was living proof that football could build bridges. She is a great example of a Penalty Taker!

How can you become a modern day pioneer?

13. Opportunity -
Walter Malone
(1866-1915)

"They do me wrong
who say I come no more -
When once I knock and fail to find you in;

For every day I stand outside your door
And bid you wake, and rise to fight and
win.

Wail not for precious chances passed away!
Weep not for golden ages on the wane!
Each night I burn the records of the day -
At sunrise every soul is born again!"

*"We are all faced with a series of great
opportunities, brilliantly disguised as
impossible situations"*
Michael Patterson

14. Overcoming the Bullies...

After freshman goalie Daniel Cui became the scapegoat for a losing season, the whole high school rallied to defend him. More than 100 students changed their profile pictures to a photo of Cui making a save. With a newfound confidence, Cui returned the next season to play the game of his life and lead his team to a win.

Although playing in goal, Daniel Cui is most definitely a Penalty Taker !

15. Do the Unexpected...

Aged 11, in the school soccer team we had a giant of a centre back, Alan Gibson was his name. Alan came from a rugby playing family and had a powerful kick that would have seemed more suited to try scoring, rather than attempting to 'bend it like Beckham'

around a wall. He was our secret weapon. We won several games and gained many points that season due to the boot of that large, imposing number five!

We would kick-off: 1st touch forward, 2nd touch back towards Alan, and then with the delicate silky skill of many 1970's centre-backs!! He would, how best can I describe it? Punt/blast/smash it toward the opposition goalkeeper, who would be way off his line, and as the football soared high above his flapping outstretched arms, there would be a memorable outcome. An astonishing, well worked, yet simple goal!

We can still gain wonderful results and achieve remarkable goals by doing the unexpected. Gibby, where are you now.....in each of our lives?

16. Apple...

 It has influenced conventional thinking within the computer industry, the small electronics industry, the

music industry, the phone industry, the broader entertainment industry and the reason is simple...

Apple starts with WHY. Apple Inspires!

17. If I Had A Million Dollars...

One of Canadian rock group Barenaked Ladies best known hits is: If I had a $1,000,000.

In football terms these days I don't suppose that would go very far, but what about within your own business? If you had $1m what could you do with it? How would it benefit your plans to expand into other markets / to introduce new products / become known as penalty takers within your industry?

Now go about sharing that vision and raise the funds to make it happen?

18. You Know What You Need to Do...

Sadly, we will achieve very little in life unless we: equip, arrange, groom, train, plan, construct, get ready, prime, put in order, make provision, draw up, develop, arrange, fashion, assemble, perfect, smooth the way ....or put simply –

 *PREPARE !*

19. The Sweet Silver Song of the Lark...

"You'll Never Walk Alone" is a show tune from the 1945 Rodgers and Hammerstein musical Carousel.

The song is also sung at association football clubs around the world, where it is performed by a mass chorus of supporters on match day; this tradition began at Liverpool Football Club in the early 1960s and has continued to be a signature tradition to present day -

"When you walk through the storm - Hold your head up high - And don't be afraid of the dark - At the end of the storm - There's a golden sky - And the sweet silver song of the lark.
Walk on, through the wind - Walk on, through the rain - Though your dreams be tossed and blown.
Walk on, walk on, with hope in your heart - And you'll never walk alone - You'll never walk alone."

No matter what challenging circumstances you're currently going through or may face, be mindful of those powerful lyrics!

20. Is Your 'Transfer' Window Broken?

Social psychologists and law enforcement officials agree: if a window in a building is broken and left in its ruined state, the rest of the windows will soon be shattered and the neighbourhood will subsequently go downhill. According to author Michael Levine, this same notion can be applied to the world of business. In "Broken Windows, Broken Business", Levine guides readers through his premise that all big dilemmas in business stem from lack of attention to small details. Using dozens of corporate "broken window" case studies, including McDonald's, K-Mart, Google, JetBlue, and more, he argues that by integrating the solutions to small problems into a much larger plan, the resulting combined solution can stimulate overall business growth-and keep customers coming back for more.

Identify the windows in your industry, office or workforce that need replaced!

21. Fergie's Way...

The final three lines in Sir Alex Fergusons 2013 autobiography simply state: "Some people when they have a holiday, they just want to go to Saltcoats, just 25 miles along the coast from Glasgow. Some people don't even want to do that, they are happy to stay at home or watch the birds and the ducks float by in the park. And some want to go to the moon."

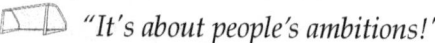 *"It's about people's ambitions!"*

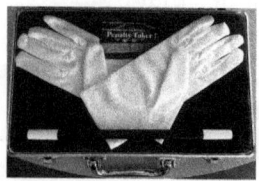

22. Make Magic Happen...

I meet with and talk about 'Penalty Takers' every single day. Penalty Takers are those who question, who become craftsmen, individuals that deliver outstanding performances. They are dynamic cyclists, vibrant starters and remarkable storytellers. Penalty Takers are martial artists, musicians and painters. They operate clapperboards, unearth gems and lead by example always. They are adventurers, scouts and mountain climbers. They step forward as sensational showstoppers, prestigious Oscar winners and life changing incredible magicians!

Go create a business full of Penalty Takers, score and achieve goal after goal - Become mighty, bold and unstoppable.

23. Getty's Formula for Success...

3 wonderfully simple and inspiring quotes from the oil billionaire J. Paul Getty:

"A man may fail many times but he isn't a failure until he begins to blame somebody else."

"If you owe the bank $100 that's your problem. If you owe the bank $100 million, that's the bank's problem."

My own personal favourite:
"Formula for success: Rise early, work hard, strike oil."

24. The Stupid Footballer is Dead...

I listened to the Audible recording of Paul's book and thoroughly enjoyed it. He talks about how professional football in the modern era is played every bit as much in the mind as on the pitch. How more and more it's becoming clear that natural talent is nowhere near enough to sustain a career in the modern game. Players need to be smart; not academically but in terms of their thinking.

Those who are dedicated, with mental resilience and a winner's psychology are prospering and will continue to do so as the game of business continues to evolve!

25. Progressing Nicely...

Create a talent program within your business or

workforce. One where your staff are encouraged to remain, that they are desirous to stay and be brilliant with you! Bottom line is………..what if they don't leave? You have trained them up to be fantastic, how great is that? Less costly, less disruptive, a succession program is vital.

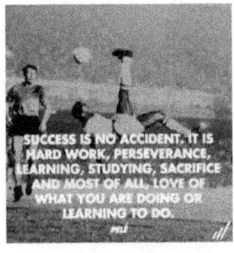 *When asked, "Who will lead tomorrow?" Feel inclined to………..leave a legacy of worth!*

26. Making the Right Pass…

1. Often the ball can be passed directly to our feet (within our comfort zone).
2. At other times, it is delivered for us to run on to (to stretch or exert ourselves).
3. A poor pass however, like one played behind, can often be the most educational: It gives us the opportunity to retrieve it from where we'd previously been. It was the wrong ball to play, misdirected, a mistake, a bad decision. We can however,

now re-group, re-focus and look to move forward once again. Not only do we learn from our own poor choices, but from the disappointing service provided by others.

 *It is often said that a wise individual learns from the mistakes of others!*
Beckham was a master ON the ball. Dalglish was a master OFF the ball.
Directly or Indirectly we can all have a powerful impact on the game of life!

27. Who Will Lead Tomorrow?

Knowing WHERE you are going and HOW to get there is vital.
Knowing WHO is travelling alongside is key.
However, ensuring continued success with the up and coming stars is how you will be remembered, that will be your true and lasting legacy.

So within your business….WHO WILL LEAD TOMORROW?

28. Keeping your Ego in Check...

If only Carlsberg made Subbuteo teams?

29. Mentor... Listen, Watch & Become...

Learn from wonderful mentors, soak up their knowledge, embrace their wisdom and then set out on a course to become one yourself!

Noun - 'An experienced and trusted adviser'.

30. Posted Missing...

Do you have a plan B, a game plan for when your two star players leave, are out injured, decide to retire or are unexpectedly transferred at short notice? Maybe, it's some key back-room staff that have chosen to seek fresh opportunities. What do you plan to do?

Occasionally we may need 'put in our place', and so it is that we also have to ensure we have contingency plans 'put in place!'

31. Pressure to Succeed...

A footballer dubbed 'the original Wayne Rooney' was tipped for stardom when Liverpool splashed out £250,000 to buy him from Oldham Athletic in 1985. The fee made Wayne Harrison the world's most expensive teenager at the age of 17, but a catalogue of injuries and logic-defying misfortune meant he never fulfilled his substantial potential.

In 1990, in the last minute of the final reserve team game of the season he collided with the Bradford City goalkeeper, tearing the cruciate ligaments in his knee. Harrison took a job as a driver and started turning out for Sunday League side Offerton Green. One pal remembers him as a 'humble, amazingly gifted man'. He said: "He started off as a substitute in the second team like everyone else and that was no problem, he had no airs or graces."

Harrison, suffered from pancreatic problems and died in hospital on Christmas Day morning 2013 aged 46.

32. Great By Choice…

Defeat is certain for him who has neglected to take the necessary precautions in time, this is called bad luck!" Roald Almundsen (Conqueror of South Pole)

"Victory awaits him who has everything in order, luck people call it!

33. Betting on Jeff...

After changing the retail industry over the past 20 years and now shaking up the publishing world, the sky truly is the limit for Jeff Bazos.

So, whether you like or dislike Amazon, the beautiful part of their story I love, is that when Bazos was looking for funding he candidly told all his original investors that there was a 70% chance that they would lose their whole stake. Even with this knowledge, his parents signed on for $300,000, a substantial portion of their life savings.

His mother stated, "we were betting on Jeff, we were investing in our son." Often that is all you need. Someone who believes in you, your product or the service you provide.

By the end of the decade, the faith his parents showed in Bezos paid off famously – as 6% owners of Amazon.com they were BILLIONAIRES!

Amazon is the world's largest online retailer and that was one impressive goal!

34. Half-Time: Heaven or Hell?

At the break, a time generally perceived to be the ideal moment to re-engage, refocus and reinvigorate your players, let me ask:

Do you go to the dressing room and receive a dressing down from whoever is in charge? Finding fault, pointing fingers and usually receiving a lengthy ten minute tirade and lecture. One which possibly totally demoralises, uninspires and drains your team of any positive energy and constructive worthwhile instruction whatsoever!

Or, on the other hand, does good fortune favour you? At the break do you head off for, and locate a changing room?

Surprisingly, 'it does exactly what it says on the tin.' It allows you room to change things, to adapt and to embrace new ways, fresh ideas and possibly mildly radical thoughts.

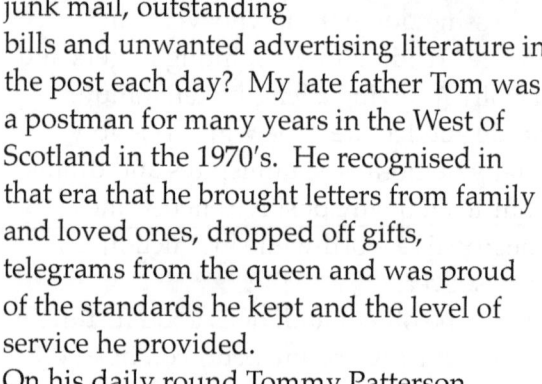 *Prepare to turn heads when you reappear, see it as an ideal opportunity to 'bounce back' and put in a breathtaking performance. Forget the first half!*

35. What Will Today Bring?

Do you only notice junk mail, outstanding bills and unwanted advertising literature in the post each day? My late father Tom was a postman for many years in the West of Scotland in the 1970's. He recognised in that era that he brought letters from family and loved ones, dropped off gifts, telegrams from the queen and was proud of the standards he kept and the level of service he provided.

On his daily round Tommy Patterson greeted his 'customers' with a smile, a vocal "good morning", and saw his job not only as a postman, but as a father – to deliver happiness to all!   He was an incredible PENALTY TAKER!

 *In each of our own demanding roles.....What do we look to deliver? How do we measure up?*

36. Class Act...

When Japan fans were pictured cleaning up rubbish in the stadium after their 2014 World Cup clash with Ivory Coast, they won plenty of applause from the football world. Their humble supporters proved it was not a one off after taking their own bin bags to the next clash with Greece – and cleaning up all over again after the full-time whistle. The supporters captured the imagination of Brazil. The Samurai army, as they are known, took their own bags and brushes to the Arena Das Dunas and used them to cheer the team on, before getting to work after the full-time whistle. They collected bottles, food wrappers and other rubbish long after thousands of other fans had left following the rather boring 0-0 draw. The supporters then neatly left the bags piled up around the back of the stands, so officials could easily dispose of them next time the bins are collected.

Those heart-warming fans helped restore pride back into the beautiful game.

In our own respective companies what do we do that sets us apart?

37. The Value of Integrity...

Defender Clive Clarke signed a three-month loan deal with Leicester City on 16 August 2007. During the League Cup tie between Nottingham Forest and Leicester on 28 August 2007, Clarke collapsed and suffered a cardiac arrest in the changing rooms at the City Ground causing the match to be abandoned at half-time, with the score at 1–0.

It was reported by the BBC that Clarke was being treated in the emergency room at the Queen's Medical Centre in Nottingham. He was said to be 'stable' and would be kept in overnight.

In an act of sportsmanship, Leicester City allowed Forest to score the opening goal on the re-match to regain the advantage they had when the first game was abandoned. Leicester players stood aside to allow Forest goalkeeper Paul Smith to walk in the ball from the kick-off. Reportedly even the bookmakers decided to pay out on the scorer of the first contested goal as well as paying out on both the 3–2 official result and the 3–1 "real" scoreline.

Clarke was 27 at the time and never played football again. After the incident he said, "he felt lucky to be alive", his heart had stopped for over four minutes.

Integrity in business is key. Hats off to Leicester City Football Club. Humble sportsmen and penalty takers one and all!

38. The Latest Best Sellers...

What novels have you bought?

What stories have you created and clung to as a way of excusing yourself from responsibility?

We are all excellent narrators. We have a story for everything.

On a daily basis does your story HELP or HINDER your growth as an individual or business?

39. Penalty Taker Extraordinaire...

In 2006 Rickie Lambert was plying his trade with Bristol Rovers in the lowly English 2nd Division. Fast-forward - and on the 12th of May 2014, Lambert was named in the 23-man England squad for the 2014 FIFA World Cup.

Then, age 32, on 2 June 2014, Lambert was confirmed as a Liverpool player after passing a medical, signing a two-year deal for an initial £4 million transfer fee plus add-ons.

Rickie Lambert was born and raised in the Westvale area of Kirkby, Merseyside. He had been released from the club as a teenager, he said

"I have always dreamt of playing for Liverpool, but I did kind of think the chance of playing for them had gone. I didn't think the chance would come again."

In only 8 seasons he climbed through all four divisions, entered into the international arena and achieved his boyhood ambition!

Speaking of which, although he never took a penalty for his first two clubs, Blackpool and Macclesfield Town, he scored 6 from 6 attempts at Stockport County, and 5 from 6 attempts for Rochdale. The single miss was against his future club, Bristol Rovers in a 2-0 win on 29 April 2006. Lambert then transferred to Rovers and continued to score well in penalties, achieving 13 goals from 14 attempts. As of the Summer 2014 his last miss to date occurred on 21 February 2009, against Leicester City in a 1-0 loss. At Southampton, in 5 full seasons he scored all 34 attempts.

How do we strive to succeed and achieve against the odds? Remember it is never too late to achieve your dreams. What an incredible story, what a determined individual and what an amazing Penalty Taker in more ways than one!

40. 'Your Song' For Today...

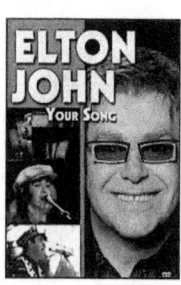

Elton John and Bernie Taupin teamed up and wrote YOUR SONG way back in 1967 and had a hit with it in 1970, and now, nearly 50 years later the lyrics resonate profoundly, especially in a business sense. We are forever using the example of others to illustrate points, quoting famous individuals and high profile figures, whilst we give presentations and share remarks.

However, in the lyrics of this song we find several relevant lines, one of which states: *"I know it's not much, but it's the best I can do – my gift is my song and this one's for you."*

Your song is THE GIFT, it's what makes life sensational. Your song is your adventures, your experiences – it's personal, it's authentic and well worth sharing. Others, like role models and mentors, absolutely play an essential part in shaping your life and inspiring you, but ultimately…GO tell YOUR STORY: Fascinate; Be Brilliant; Influence; Be a Gulliver and go change the world!

Then in the words of Bernie Taupin: "You can tell everybody this is YOUR SONG and then remind them - How wonderful life is while you're in the world."

Be a Penalty Taker – and go create a symphony of work to share today, tomorrow and for years to come.

41. Iconic, just like Seth...

Lessons from the Eiffel Tower.
A post by iconic marketer Seth Godin –

Enjoy!

* It was designed at home, on the kitchen table by someone who didn't get their name on it.
* Never been done before, not guaranteed to get built or to work.
* It was criticized by hundreds of leading intellectuals and cultural experts.
* It was not supposed to last very long.
* It is designed to be an icon, it's not an accident.
* People flock to it because it is famous.
* You can sketch a recognizable version of it on a napkin.

Now it is your turn to build one, what will it look like?

42. The Fans...

Barry Sweeney said he feared the worst when he heard about the plane coming down. Two Newcastle United fans going to the club's pre-season tour were on the flight that crashed in the Ukraine. John Alder and Liam Sweeney, 28, were both on the passenger list for flight MH17, Malaysia Airlines confirmed. The Boeing 777 from Amsterdam to Kuala Lumpur crashed on Thursday 17th July 2014 with 298 people on board.

Newcastle United and then manager Alan Pardew paid tribute to the fans. The two men were travelling to New Zealand to see their team play. Liam Sweeney's father, Barry, praised the response of Newcastle United after it was announced players would wear black armbands in upcoming games in tribute to the two fans. Newcastle's then managing director Lee Charnley described the news as "devastating."

He said:

"Both men were dedicated supporters of our club and were known to thousands of fans and staff alike. "On behalf of everyone at Newcastle United we send our deepest condolences to John and Liam's families and friends."

Alan Pardew said: "Myself and all the players are deeply shocked and saddened by this terrible news. We all knew how passionately John and Liam supported the team and the club. They were with us just earlier this week for our first pre-season friendly against Oldham and their dedication to travel all the way around the world to support us in New Zealand tells you all you need to know about the passion they had for Newcastle United." Newcastle United said Mr Alder was a lifelong supporter and a familiar sight in the stands for almost half a century, having barely missed a single game in that time. Fanzine The Mag, said:

"It is a tragedy though for all Newcastle fans and we hope everybody, whether they knew them or not, gives a minute to think about their loss, as well as all of those other people who tragically lost their lives on that flight."

Taking the time to show our respect, our appreciation and our gratitude to those individuals and groups that support us, buy our products or use our services is the very least we can do in this busy turbulent world that we live in. To recognise those that sustain us through the hard times as well as the good. Communicating with our fans, supporters and consumers is easier than at any time in our history. However, let us not always wait for the tragedies to unfold, the negative or poor customer relation experiences to come to the fore. Acknowledge them in numerous, innovative and original ways as many companies and businesses currently do! Engage early, creating close personal and interactive relationships with fans, both locally, nationally and internationally. Through various aspects of social media they become important components within the team, they have a vital role to play, one which has a common goal, focused and with a united purpose, a synergy that can drive forward success.

As a supporter, enthusiast, devotee, follower or admirer, ask yourself – how would you like to be treated? Then do so accordingly!

43. Constructive Advice...

...may not be what you want to hear, but it is often what you REALLY need to hear.

Not make believe or concocted, but practical. Not based on making you feel **<u>uneasy</u>**, but for you to become **<u>unbelievable</u>**.

Phil Neville took plenty of abuse for his media work throughout the World Cup in Brazil 2014.

Constructive feedback is vital and it is not given to make you feel better, but designed to... MAKE YOU BETTER.

I am not sure which is most courageous... giving it or receiving it?

Go search for it and welcome with open arms the bold colleagues and honest friends who love you enough to offer it.

44. Rise Early and Strike Oil...

Productivity tip: from people who get things done.

📓 *"I get up around 4.30am and naturally the first thing I do is make some coffee."*
Howard Schultz (Starbucks Chairman, President and CEO)

45. Step up to the Mark...

There is no escaping everyday anxiety.
So harness it positively.

📓 *Become a Penalty Taker in business and in life!*

46. Sound Help...

A good coach is someone who understands you, challenges you, and is a person you can count on to pat you on the back and get you back on the pitch when you stumble!

Be someone who can give correction without causing resentment.

47. Popular or Not...

Growing up as a music fan in the 70's and 80's, a staple diet of Top of the Pops on the TV and The Charts on the radio at the week-end would be my regular music catch up.
When I purchase music, films or books online these days, I am normally confronted with a list, which can be

alphabetical, but it is normally the most popular. Now, I recognise that when I listen to the top 40, review the dvd chart or bestsellers list, that others are deciding for me what I want to hear, watch and read. Most people only read bestselling books, that's what makes them bestsellers after all. The web defaults to 'sort by popular,' throwing up hit, after hit, after hit.

It's likely many of the concepts, notions and services we utilise in daily life, are actually being used because, in the words of a song from the musical Wicked, they are the most 'POPULAR'.

In football, with the right financial resources, it is easy to go out and buy those individuals currently performing well, on the top of their game, or those who recently impressed in a few World Cup matches. In business - work colleagues who have performed well in recent years and are known in the industry can be enticed from competing firms, etc.

However, it takes real dedication, thought and preparation to seek out alternatives that are less apparent, where the option is a bit more uncertain, fraught with an element of danger, intrigue and surprise. Louis Van Gaal swopped goalkeepers with 30 seconds to go – unheard of, unbelievable and in many parts unpopular.

Don't let others choose – Decide for yourself. Go find those hidden treasures, be surprised and delighted, experience something new and discover your own identity!

48. Take the Spot Kick...

Don't be afraid to fail. Within that experience, you will find some of the best lessons life can give you!

49. Scarce, Because it's Difficult...

Shortly after the 2014 World Cup finished, Javier Mascherano voiced his admiration for Barcelona team-mate Lionel Messi and believes his countryman is the best of his generation.

High praise indeed from a professional whose role in the Argentina side often went unnoticed to the untrained eye. His role required him to do extremely difficult work and that added value to the team's performance. It was not a role that most people could perform well in, or adapt easily too.

In business it should seem obvious then, right?

Produce a product or service that is valued but scarce because it's difficult, and you're more likely to be sought after and better rewarded for what you do.

The suggestion is simple, yet incredible. When outlining a new scheme or mastering a talent, look for the most challenging area to become an expert in and ... if it's easy, then it's not for you!

50. Made To Last?

Pele , Beckenbauer and Cruyff's silky skills, classic style and sheer originality have survived fittingly over these past 30 to 40 years. Not unlike Willie Nelson, Johnny Cash, Waylon Jennings and Kris Kristofferson who collectively played together as The Highwaymen in the mid nineteen eighties. Many of the songs that they wrote back then have stood the test of time admirably. What do you currently produce?
How will it stand up to scrutiny in 30 years? What do you or your firm contribute?

Each of the Highwaymen were recognised as established experts within the music industry, a top performer, a renowned singer or songwriter. However, they were willing to join forces, to share and collaborate in partnership. Setting aside huge egos and differences, they each contributed positively and strongly to their musical union.

Reflecting on the legacy we can leave, and how it may still be relevant in three decades time, ask yourself…Do you have star performers in the workplace? Colleagues that could join forces, put their heads together and discern if they could streamline, be more efficient, utilise and combine their individual strengths and procedures, so as to become stronger, more resolute and better positioned to face the ever changing demands of business and life in the 21st Century?

 *Worth considering!*

51. In Three Words or Less…

Just Three Words

If the objective was for your business, company, product or service to be recognised in three words or less, how would you do? What would they be? Possibly a star player, performer or figurehead, how would you describe them?

Man in Black: The King and Apple are just a few that come to mind that when uttered, the majority of people know who they are or what they refer to.

What mantra, slogan or tag makes you stand out from the crowd? How can you promote it, push it or instill it as a brand worth remembering?

52. The Dutch Bathroom...

Back in the Summer of 2008, just as the UEFA European Football Championships were about to take place, my wife and daughter headed off on an overnight camping trip with a group of other youth and their leaders.

I have three children and my oldest, Gordon was in South London at this time and with Jennifer accompanying her mum, that left my youngest son Andrew and I to our own devices. Well, rather than get up to anything mischievous, we decided that we could surprise his mother and sister by painting our bathroom. The room had never been decorated since we had moved into our cottage property four years earlier, this was the perfect opportunity.

With regards to the football, I had chosen the Netherlands, Holland, the mighty Dutch as my favourites to win Euro 2008. They played a graceful passing game, had many top players plying their skills around the globe and most importantly …….. I loved their bright colourful strips!

You may have already guessed it, but when mother and daughter arrived home on the Saturday morning, they were greeted to a newly emulsioned bathroom, complete with three large circular floor mats in a matching shade, the colour being 'delicious' ORANGE! It was bold, striking and extremely bright…sun glasses were provided on the bathroom shelf as you entered.

Sometimes in business and in life…..we just make mistakes!!!!

The opportunity then presents itself, to pick ourselves up, to learn a lesson and grow, to take full responsibility and possibly correct our actions (the bathroom was repainted white). As we move forward we learn to communicate more clearly and include other key decision makers in our vision for the future!

53. The Mighty Irn Bru...

Success often comes in ways we least expect!
I once had the wonderful opportunity to share a presentation with some fantastic business people at an Edinburgh Chamber of Commerce breakfast.
A wide range of members were represented from bankers, accountants and media specialists, to self-employed, writers and coaches. There was a definite early morning buzz of excitement being generated in the room, a vibrancy that was being encouraged with the beautiful warm ray of sunshine that streamed in through the Edinburgh skyline.

Having experienced numerous business events over the years, you are not always as a guest fully aware of what is coming up next, even with a timetable or schedule in hand. Occasionally your thoughts may turn to who, how and in what manner is this workshop or seminar going to be delivered?

With regards to our chamber breakfast, I suspect 100% of the chamber members were totally unaware of what would happen next.

Just four days previously I had been working on a business presentation dealing with company brands, their logos and slogans. I was correlating this, when a piece of music that was playing on my iPod caught my attention. It was an instrumental Scottish/Irish medley and was foot tapping and infectious! At first I started to whistle and then I began to hum to the music, finally I began to sing along. However, instead of the normal lyrics associated with the tunes, I began substituting some of the world's top global brands into the song, this was - NOT AS EXPECTED!

Sixty minutes later the full medley had 'brand' new lyrics, I had no intention of using it soon, it had simply been highly invigorating creating it. The experience lifted my mood, set me up with a smile and spring in my step for the rest of the day. So when it came time to prepare and write down some ideas for the chamber breakfast, 'The Brand Song' kept coming back into my mind. It's formation, it's origin, it's emergence and how it came about, illustrate my point perfectly.

It was not as expected!

How often in life as we grow as individuals, as our companies develop and hopefully we achieve a level of success both in business and in life, do we take time out to reflect, to review and ponder on how our voyage having left A and ultimately having arrived at B, was not as expected! Guaranteed it will not have been 'as the crow flies', but with a variety of detours, set backs and surprising decisions we had not foreseen, certainly -

Not as Expected!

From the seeds of a business idea to multi national global brand, it started somewhere! You had a path, a road to travel, an exciting journey ahead. How many times did the route change? You ventured down side streets, dead ends and avenues, before returning with greater expectations and a clearer and more precise vision of exactly what you wanted to achieve. Even the final destination may have altered, as you refined the idea, recognised it's true potential, then looked out your passport and took it to parts of the world you had never dreamed possible previously.

That morning **Not As Expected** I sang 'The Mighty Irn Bru', as I had since entitled it. I then shared thoughts on how as we strive to set targets and goals in our lives and achieve our ambitions, that we will be remarkably surprised, shocked and astonished at how they have come about.

Evaluate, study and review your own journey, don't be taken aback at how your success and triumph has came about ....NOT AS EXPECTED!

54. Kick Off: The Game...

Penalty Takers:

Mentors, Role Models, Examples, Styles, Values and Approaches to the game. Getting you to give some quality thinking to your staff and their skill set, what they bring to the job and the role they currently play, or the potential new position you envisage for them.

You don't always know the cards you'll be dealt in life, ultimately it is how you cope with challenges, mishaps or potential opportunities that will help you succeed in business and life, 'when the whistle blows.'

From 50 colleagues, dismiss 26 and name 24 in your original squad ... then choose your final 16. Difficult decision leaving behind 33% of the group.

Then on match day, another third go, name your starting eleven. Straightforward... really?

At the end of season you have been bought over, staff will have to merge, new jobs, less roles, who knows? Discuss, persuade, act! Decision reached - Downsize required. New, leaner, fitter 5-a-side team required to build upon for next year/ what characters traits are you after, likely to embrace, what do you require to move you forward and up the league table in the coming season ahead?
Who from your 11 will survive the cut, another 50% need to go. So who will make your final five?

With 90% of the players now gone, who are the Penalty Takers you have chosen to surround yourself with? Who has made your TOP 10%.

- Understanding, creating and training for specific roles.
- Having a clear vision for tomorrow, by nurturing and investing in the future.
- Outside influences, disciplinary issues, media attention and pressure, transfers, back from injury, scoring regularly, stars of

tomorrow, near misses, goals,
transfers to and from clubs,
managers leaving, etc, etc.

*Intriguing, thought provoking and it
certainly gets the discussion flowing. There
would appear to be much more to being a
penalty taker than just kicking the ball!
Who would be starting in your team and why?*

55. Creating Customer Loyalty...

*Every 20 seconds, of
every day, Real Madrid sell
one of these!*

56. Often the Briefest of Moments...

I had the delightful
pleasure several years
ago of travelling from my
beautiful home on the
outskirts of Edinburgh,

Scotland, to visit Colonial Williamsburg in Virginia, USA.

Whilst perusing around one of their many gift shops, I came across a beautiful, small, antique style wooden plaque, which had a faded picture printed across its front. It was the side of a log cabin, with an opening about half way up where a frame containing four equal panes of glass were positioned.

Emblazoned on the plaque in bold lettering was the word OPPORTUNITY.

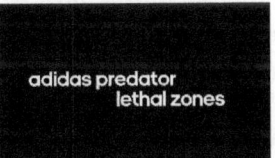 *Underneath it a smaller inscription simply read, "always look for your window of opportunity!"*

57. Making Every Touch Count. Part 2

adidas predator
lethal zones

A game is 90 minutes long. Broken down, stats show that is equal to 90 seconds on the ball, which equates to roughly 60-80 ball contacts.

It means every touch you have on the ball needs to count! Dribble; First Touch; Sweet Spot; Control & Pass and Drive are the 5 lethal zone areas. The players have to be behind the concept; live the concept and ultimately love the concept!

In business what are your Lethal Zones?

58. Are You Becoming Legendary?

In life, football and business, we often face hurdles and obstacles throughout the course of the game. Relating back to his family roots in his 2013 autobiography, Sir Alex reminds us that the Ferguson clan motto is: 'Dulcius Ex Asperis' - Sweeter After Difficulties.

An apt reminder to face up to the challenges we face on a daily basis. To see them as opportunities to learn, grow and develop and to appreciate the moment of triumph more fully when it arrives.

59. High Calibre Penalty Takers…

When we look at pictures of celebrities as young children, toddlers, even in their early teens, we do not recognise them. Nobody knew them or was aware of them at that stage in their life. But, as they grew, developed purpose, discovered what they wanted from life and what they could offer, knew what they desired to achieve, what was required and why.

They then became enchanting, skillful accomplished performers, masters of brilliance.

Hard work, effort and numerous exciting ideas would come and go. The unseen hours, the research, the failures – then back to the drawing board, produce three cups, one ball, where did it go? Creating more magic…changing lives and changing the world …Forever!

Several years ago when I got married and went on holiday, it became a standing joke that one of my suitcases would contain one or all of the following: Large ghetto blaster, whole host of cd's, a camera with several rolls of film and flash bulbs. Also, the case would contain: boxed games, quiz magazines and other publications, a selection of books, refill pads, pens and coloured pencils.

Now, like so many of you, I carry all that ESSENTIAL stuff in my pocket, it's my phone! Oh, and for good measure: it's a TV, video recorder, dictaphone. I message people instantly, send postcards from the bath, it's a mail order catalogue on demand, it allows face to face chats with family in Outer Mongolia & hundreds of other functions, that no doubt I have still to figure out.
Oh, and it can also tell the time too!

Magic, Abracadabra…Hey Presto….Lives are different now, countries and cultures have had to adjust, the world has changed.

Later people recognised Steve Jobs, Bill Gates and Mark Elliot Zuckerberg, because of who they grew up to become. Individuals that influenced and ultimately changed the world. In my sporting terminology – they were Penalty Takers of the highest calibre!

In order for each of us to change the world, our choice is relatively simple.
Go be someone!

Grow up and become a wonderful parent, a faithful friend, a trusted colleague. Become more knowledgeable, study and train, become a highly skilled professional, a loving grandparent. Become a contagious individual, that people can't helped catch your infectious goodness, your vitality for life, your generosity of spirit. They will have no option but to share those powerful qualities, to smile at others, interact and become a leader also. Via modern technology and your condition …YOU WILL GO VIRAL !

Becoming would imply, 'begins to be' – So what are you going to 'begin to be' and ultimately 'Become?' From a business perspective, what do you want to become? What does the future look like? What are you going to revolutionize and how are you now going to change the world?

Learn the moves required, perform at your best and then generously sprinkle some magic and go "Become the Someone You Were Meant to Be."

60. Coming out of the Shadows...

The Milestones
Jock Stein CBE (1922-1985)

A fitting tribute in word and verse,
I would like to tell to you,
about a man that was born on the 5th of
October, in the year of 1922.

Raised and brought up in Burnbank,
Hamilton, in a clean and humble abode.
The only son of George and Jean, at three,
three, nine on the Glasgow Road.

In '37' he left Greenfield School in search of
something finer,
a brief period within a carpet factory and
then on to become a miner.
Then arrived the year of '42', an ambition
fulfilled soon to be,
for he became a professional football player
and signed for Albion Rovers F.C.

In '50', it was Wales and Llanelly Town,
not knowing shortly his work there would
be done,
he then signed for the great Glasgow Celtic
in the December of 1951.
Going on to become club captain and
always pushing and striving for more,
he then guided them to the League and
Cup double, in the year of '54'.

In 1956 due to injury, retirement would
leave him feeling numb,
but little did the fans and players know,
that his day was yet to come!

On the 14th of March 1960, he took charge
of Dunfermline F.C.
That was soon to become the platform, to
show just how special he would be.

In '61', they lifted the Scottish Cup, a fine
start to his managerial career.
For a club so long in the wilderness, it
became a wonderful, classic, great year.
'62' and they ventured to Europe, with
games in the Inter-Cities Cup,
could he have foretold that in only five
years,
a different trophy – he would then hold up.

April '64' has arrived and a short stint at
Hibernian proved to be fun,
within months of arriving at Easter Road,
yet another trophy was won.
March nineteen hundred and sixty five,
now manager of Celtic F.C.
Within weeks the Scottish Cup is captured,
the start of much silverware we are about
to see.

The special year was soon to arrive, in '67'
they played with a passion and a pride,
winners of every competition they entered,

European Cup holders, the first British
side.
In '70' the European Cup final again,
although against Feyenoord it was not to
be,
but a medal still did arrive in this year, in
the shape of the honours list - a C.B.E.

A low point was on the horizon, and soon
it did arrive,
whilst returning home from holiday – the
car crash of seventy five.
In '77' the Premier League Championship
was captured yet again,
in his time with the club it was now to
become, League title number ten.

Now one year later in '78', things they were
hectic, so much going on –
A testimonial, Leeds and the Scotland job,
from his beloved Celtic Park he was gone.
By '82' we had qualified for the World Cup
Finals once again
and those in the party he had taken as
boys, no doubt returned home as men.

There was just nine minutes remaining
and Davie Cooper stepped up to keep our
hopes alive,
well aware of the tension packed
atmosphere on the 10th of September '85.
It's there, it's gone in, he has slid the ball
home,
just as calmly as if he was in training.
The Welsh spirit was crushed and they
offered no threat,
in the final few minutes remaining.

Amid the dancing and jubilation, a grey
cloud was to darken the skies,
it became apparent from the fans grief
twisted faces and the T.V. presenters eyes:

Jock Stein had died that evening,
the nations manager now was gone.
Scots huddled, silent, with tear stained
faces -
to this day his memory lives on!

*His legacy remains strong over thirty
years later. Will yours?*

61. Start Something that Matters...

Blake Mycoskie first visited Argentina with his sister in 2002. He returned there on vacation in January 2006, and noticed that the local polo players were wearing a form of shoes called alpargatas, a simple canvas slip-on shoe that he himself began to wear.

The shoes have been worn by Argentine farmers for hundreds of years and were the inspiration for the classic style of Toms shoes. Later in the trip, when he was doing some volunteer work in the outskirts of Buenos Aires, he noticed that many of the children were running through the streets barefooted. After discovering that a lack of shoes was a wider problem in Argentina and other developing countries than just this one community, he decided that he wanted to develop a kind of alpargata for the North American market, with the caveat that for every pair sold he would provide a new pair of shoes free of charge to the shoeless youth of Argentina and other developing nations.

He took the idea to Argentine shoe manufacturers and began building the company based on this idea, and initially made 250 pairs of shoes. The company first officially began selling its shoes in May 2006. After an article ran in the Los Angeles Times, the company received order requests for nine times the available stock online, and 10,000 pairs were sold in the first six months. The first batch of free shoes were distributed in October 2006.

The company was self-financed, as Mycoskie sold his online driver education company for $500,000 to fund the shoe company. The company name (TOMS) is derived from the word "tomorrow," and evolved from the original concept, "Shoes for Tomorrow Project."

By 2011 over 500 retailers were carrying the brand globally; that year it also launched its eyewear line. By 2012 over two million pairs of new shoes had been given to children in developing countries around the world. In June 2014, the company announced that founder Blake Mycoskie was looking to sell part of his stake in the company to investment partners in a move to help grow and expand faster and meet the long-term goals of the company.

On August 20, 2014 it was announced that Bain Capital had acquired 50% of Toms. Reuters reported that the transaction valued the company at $625 million. Mycoskie retained 50% ownership of Toms, as well as his role as Chief Shoe Giver, and said that the goal of the sale was to build the company's global impact. Mycoskie will use half of the proceeds from the sale to start a new fund to support socially minded entrepreneurship, and Bain will match his investment and continue the company's one-for-one policy.

Author Daniel H. Pink described the company's business model as "expressly built for purpose maximization," whereby Toms is both selling shoes and selling its ideal; creating consumers that are purchasing shoes and also making a purchase that transforms them into benefactors—a company goal if it is not a consumer goal.

The company's shoe distribution partners have focused on distributing shoes in areas where the health and social benefits of the shoes would be the highest. For example, in Ethiopia the shoes are intended to help prevent a soil-borne disease that attacks the lymphatic system and which largely affected women and children.Toms sunglasses are sold with the One for One model, however it does not necessarily provide glasses only to citizens of developing countries. The One for One model includes putting money towards medical treatment and eye surgeries, in addition to prescription glasses.

The canvas shoes have been given to children in 40 countries worldwide, including the United States, Argentina, Ethiopia, Rwanda, Swaziland, Guatemala, Haiti, South Africa. Toms are sold at more than 500 stores nationwide and internationally.

Volunteers on shoe distribution trips are able to hand-deliver shoes to children. In

2006, Toms distributed 10,000 pairs of shoes in Argentina. In November 2007, the company distributed 50,000 pairs of shoes to children in South Africa. As of April 2009, Toms had distributed 140,000 pairs of shoes to children in Argentina, Ethiopia, South Africa as well as children in the United States.

As of 2012, Toms has given away over one million pairs of shoes in 40 countries.

 *Go start something that matters today!*

 ## 62. Change Direction...

"Character isn't something you were born with and cannot change like your fingerprint. It is something you weren't born with and must take responsibility for forming." Jim Rohn.

Go where the expectations are so strong that they motivate you, push you, urgently insist that you not remain in the same place!

63. Your Words Matter, Choose Carefully...

Seth Godin

Seth Godin (Marketing guru) grounds what he says with very powerful examples. Whenever he makes a point, he uses strategically chosen examples to illustrate what he's talking about. He doesn't say, "You should, or you must," no, he's not preaching. He says, "Josiah Wedgwood was born as a poor potter and would have died poor. However, he noticed that there is an industrial revolution taking place, took appropriate action, and ended up with more money in his bank account than Bill Gates." Now you're listening.

Also worth noticing is that he doesn't initiate his examples explicitly - for example, he doesn't say, "Meet Josiah Wedgwood" or "Enter Josiah Wedgwood."

Such introductory phrases would require your attention and effort - in effect, he would lose momentum.

 *Pull out the relevant facts right from the start and tell the story.*

64. Walk Tall...

In 1964 Irish singer Val Doonican had a hit single with the song Walk Tall. The chorus of which is:
Walk tall, walk straight and look the world right in the eye.
That's what my mama told me when I was about knee high.
She said, son, be a proud man and hold your head up high.
Walk tall, walk straight and look the world right in the eye.

Each of us have the opportunity to be a GIANT amongst men...

G - <u>Generous</u> & <u>Gracious</u>
I - <u>Inspiring</u> & <u>Impactful</u>
A - <u>Appreciative</u> & <u>Acknowledging</u>
N - <u>Nurturing</u> & <u>Natural</u>
T - <u>Tantalizing</u> & <u>Truthful</u>

Be bold in your vision, rise and stand tall above the crowd and be outstanding in all that you do!

65. To Charm, Delight and Enrapture...

How do companies such as Apple create such enchanting products? And how do some people always seem to enchant others?

According to bestselling business guru Guy Kawasaki, anyone can learn the art of enchantment. It transforms situations and relationships, turns cynics into believers, and changes hearts and minds.

What does 'enchantment' look like in your business?

66. Perseverance & Success...

The Alchemist by Paulo Coelho, was first released by an obscure Brazilian publishing house. Albeit having sold "well", the publisher of the book told Coelho that it was never going to sell, and that "he could make more money in the stock exchange". Needing to "heal" himself from this setback, Coelho set out to leave Rio de Janeiro with his wife and spent 40 days in the Mojave Desert. Returning from the excursion, Coelho decided he had to keep on struggling. Coelho was "so convinced it was a great book that [he] started knocking on doors".

The Alchemist has been translated into 67 distinct different languages according to The New York Times. This gave Coelho the position as the world's most translated living author, according to the 2009 Guinness World Records.

> *Those who succeed owe their success to diligence, hard work and perseverance. Continue to 'knock on doors', have faith and confidence in your product and 'don't give up!'*

67. Why Walk When You Can Fly?

Songwriter Mary Chapin Carpenter is a great favourite of mine, and she has stated in recent years, "songwriting has always been this way of expressing things to the world and to myself. Language is a magical thing and whether it is put to music or not, it takes you places.......why walk when you can fly?"

> *What new heights can you reach? It is truly possible to become the best at doing what you love!*

68. Become a Hero to Your Son...

The actions of others should inspire us into action! British comedian John Bishop raised money for individuals in Sierra Leone as part of the Sport Relief efforts in the first quarter of 2012. During his 5 day endurance test, Bishop cycled from Paris to Calais, then rowed across the English Channel to Dover. He then ran 3 marathons in 3 days, finishing in London. There was over £2m pledged.

When John Bishop finished his grueling challenge, he was greeted like a national hero. He had changed, and he had helped to save many lives.
As John crossed the finishing line, his youngest son Daniel remarked, "He will always be my dad, but now he is my hero."

Complete the task in hand and inspire others through your actions and become that hero!

69. Life: A Sublime Odyssey...

Yip Harburg
(1896-1981), who was a popular American song lyricist (inc. "Somewhere Over the Rainbow") stated: "I am one of the last of a small tribe of troubadours, who still believe that life is a beautiful and exciting journey, with a purpose and grace well worth singing about."

Is your mantra or mission statement as sincere, simple and succinct?

70. Instivate - To INSpire, moTIVate and educATE...

Check: www.coursera.org & www.edx.org
Explore short educational courses from 4 to 12 weeks and longer.
Offered by the worlds top universities.

Absolutely free of charge!

71. Fishing For Leaders...

There is a fish in Japan called the koi. You put a koi fish in a fishbowl and give it all the food and water you want to give it, but it never grows to more than about two inches in size. But, if you take the koi fish out of the fish bowl and throw it in a pond somewhere, the koi fish grows to about a foot in size.

The moral of the story is that the koi fish grows proportionately to the environment in which it lives. Leaders understand this premise and principle and create for others the kind of environment in which, through which, and by which others are willing to excel and grow and be nurtured and nourished.

Help others to develop within their surroundings. Give them the autonomy, authority and backing to grow and fulfill their potential!

72. The Impact of the Highly Improbable...

Nassim Nicolas Taleb in recent years wrote a book in which he uses the term Black Swan to define, "any event that occurs outside the realm of expectation." For a long time, Europeans believed that all swans were white. Then when Australia was discovered, so too was a species of swans that were black! Not only did the discovery of Australia change the perception of the world, but also peoples' perception of swans had to change.

The book is all about the random events that underlie our lives, from bestsellers to world disasters. Their affect is huge; they're nearly impossible to predict; yet after they happen we always try to rationalize them.

A rallying cry to ignore the 'experts'. The Black Swan shows us how to stop trying to predict everything and take advantage of uncertainty.

73. Greetings From...

One of my close friends recently went off to walk the North Devon Coastal Path, I was bemused to receive a postcard which showed a glorious view of cliffs and sea, but which only bore the message:

"This trip is just like life."

On his return he gave me the explanation. "The journey was certainly full of interest," he told me, "But, it was equally full of ups and downs. Every time I managed to successfully slog my way up a hill, I was rewarded by the most glorious vistas – and by the satisfaction of being able to look back to see just how far I'd come."

 *Remind yourself that there are wonderful views which await those who don't give up!*

74. Wait Until Wednesday...

Worries – we all have them. But perhaps we sometimes have a tendency to worry for no good reason.

I like the story of the late millionaire businessman and film producer, J. Arthur Rank. Having little time to waste he decided that he would do all his worrying on the one day – Wednesday.

Each time a worry loomed Mr Rank would write it down on a piece of paper, fold it, slip it into a wooden box and forget about it until the following Wednesday. The amazing thing was that when he opened the box again most of the things he might have spent time fretting over had already taken care of themselves.

Try it for yourself, choose a day that works for you!

75. On a Positive Note...

For several years
in their youth, each
of our children went to the British
Accordion Championships, held annually
at that time in Scarborough, England.
This one year I listened to a young fourteen
year old named Alan play his elementary
piece. All went well until he made a
mistake in the third verse.
Later he lamented to his mother that his
one wrong note had ruined the tune. His
wise parent quickly replied, "That's not
true at all! It's the other five hundred and
odd perfect notes that you played which
everyone will remember."

*Starting today, turn your self-criticism
into self- appreciation. You'll feel the difference
immediately!*

76. Three Little Words...

When Dr. David Livingstone (1813-1873) was a young man, there were three words he was warned never to use - "I DON'T CARE" The person who warned him explained why. "You will start by saying 'I don't care' about little things – a message you forgot to pass on, a letter you ought to have written, a plate that you broke. Before you know it you will be saying you don't care about things that really matter. You will let your friends down. You will make mistakes and not bother to put them right."

"Never say 'I don't care'. Say YOU DO CARE – and mean it."

77. Life is an Exciting Business...

Alone we can do so little; together we can do so much."

Helen Keller

Imagine being deaf, dumb and blind.

Helen Keller, a healthy baby born in 1880 in Alabama, contracted a fever when only 19 months old. The short illness left her totally blind and deaf.

As an adult she toured America raising funds for the American Foundation for the Blind and campaigned for people with disabilities like hers who were often housed in asylums.

This inspirational woman, despite being faced with seemingly insurmountable problems, discovered a great secret.

"Life is an exciting business," she said. "And it is most exciting when it is lived for others."

We ask ourselves, who am I to be brilliant, gorgeous, handsome, talented and fabulous? Actually, who are you not to be?

Nelson Mandela

meetville.com

78. Our Deepest Fear...

No one would have been surprised if Nelson Mandela had emerged from his years of captivity a bitter man, but instead he turned inward, examining his soul, and finding moral courage and insight. It is from him that we receive these words of encouragement:

"Our worst fear is not that we are inadequate. Our deepest fear is that we are powerful beyond measure. It is our light, not our darkness that most frightens us. We ask ourselves, 'Who am I to be brilliant, gorgeous, talented and fabulous?' Actually, who are you not to be? You are a child of God: your playing small doesn't serve the world. There is nothing enlightened about shrinking so that other people won't feel insecure around you. We were born to make manifest the glory of God within us. It is not just in some of us, it is in everyone, and as we let our own light shine, we unconsciously give other people permission to do the same. As we are liberated from our own fear, our presence automatically liberates others."

Free others by being brilliant, be all that you can be!

79. Would You Like to Go Large With That?

AFTER YEARS OF HARD WORK AT MC DONALDS
I FINALLY MANAGED TO BUY A CAMERA

The High School teacher would call out the roll at the start of class:
Fleming, Ian, here; Francis, Stuart, here; Gallagher, John, and just at that the bold John Gallagher rushed through the door late as always.

He was the class clown, he liked to show off and was immature. He never recognised just how important it was to get good qualifications. He had no set plans for his future and at that point no idea what he wanted from life. Sound familiar?
Let me tell you Johns Story: In the mid seventies aged just 16 he began working WITH McDonald's part time. At 18 on leaving school he began full time employment. At 21 he became a Supervisor, 22 a Trainee Manager and an Assistant Manager at age 24.

After two more years, aged 26, he became a Store Manager. He had learned the trade, served his time, a decade of experience now behind him.

At age 29 he became an Area Manager and after three more years of understanding the business more fully, gaining a better understanding of the product, the pricing and policies, he became a Franchise Owner at only 32 years of age. Aged 35 he bought his second franchise and five years later, as a forty year old he purchased store number three!

In 2006, John sold his three franchises for **£8.5 million.**

He paid off £3.5 million in outstanding loans. With £5 million in the bank he retired from the fast food industry at age 45!

No matter the business - Working WITH, rather than FOR...will make all the difference!

80. Be a Showstopper...

and teach the world to sing.

The products and services you want to sell will not succeed in the market if you don't address the emotional wants of 'real people.' It is not enough these days just to fulfill the material needs of 'prospects'. A business (your business) needs to look past the labels it gives the people it serves, and see their hopes, dreams, fears and aspirations.

On the 11th of April 2009, the sniggering began as soon as the plump, matronly woman walked onto the stage. She looked more like a lunch lady than a vocalist. First, she was too old to be competing on Britain's Got Talent, having just turned forty-seven, ten days earlier on April Fool's Day, she was more than twice the age of many of the other contestants.

But, more important, she looked, well, frumpy. The other competitors were already dressed to be the next big thing.

Sexy, ruggedly handsome or hip. They wore figure hugging dresses, tailored tops and summer scarves . But this woman looked more like an example of what not to wear. Her outfit looked like a cross between an old set of curtains and a secondhand Easter dress.

  And she was nervous. When the judges started asking her questions she got stuck and stumbled on her words. "What's the dream?" they inquired. When she replied that she wanted to be a professional singer you could just see the thoughts going through their heads. That's rich! You? A professional singer? The cameras zoomed in on members of the audience laughing and rolling their eyes. Even the judges smirked. They clearly wanted her to get off the stage as soon as possible. All signs pointed to her giving a terrible performance and being booted from the show, pronto.

But just as it seemed that it couldn't get any worse, she started singing.

And time stopped. It was breathtaking.

As the opening chords from "I Dreamed a Dream" from Les Miserables wafted over the speakers, Susan Boyle's exquisite voice shone through like a beacon. So powerful, so beautiful that it made the hair on the back of your neck stand up. The judges were in awe, the audience screamed and everyone broke out into wild applause. Some started tearing up as they listened. The performance left people speechless.

Susan Boyle's first appearance on Britain's Got Talent is one of the most viral videos ever. In just nine short days, the clip accumulated more than 100 million views. How would you like a small taste of that kind of marketing?

It's hard to watch this video and not be encouraged by her strength, passion and heart. It's not only moving, it's inspiring. She sang on behalf of everyone whose hope, dream and aspiration it was to be on that stage, she connected and engaged with the viewer, and that emotion drove people to pass it on.

This illustrates the point perfectly that when you build an audience, you don't have to buy people's attention - they give it to you. This is a huge advantage.

 *So build an audience....Speak, write, blog, tweet, make videos, whatever. Share information that's valuable and you'll surely build a loyal following. Then when you need to get the word out, the right people will be listening.*

81. Ready, Steady, Cook...

A signature dish is a recipe that identifies an individual chef. Ideally it should be unique and allow an informed gastronome to name the chef in a blind tasting. It can be thought of as the culinary equivalent of an artist finding their own style, or an author finding their own voice. Let's look to leave aside the main course and the dessert for now.

Concentrate on being a small dish taken before a meal to stimulate one's appetite.....Become a STARTER!

82. A Guide to Cross Selling...

There were fewer than 3000 cars in France over 100 years ago when two tyre manufacturers decided to publish a guide for French motorists. It was intended to boost the demand for vehicles, and thus for car tyres.

The brothers had nearly 35,000 copies printed in 1900. It was then given away free of charge, and contained useful information for motorists, including maps, instructions for repairing and changing tyres, lists of car mechanics, hotels and petrol stations. Four years later the siblings published a similar guide for Belgium. In 2013 the guide was published in 14 editions and sold in nearly 90 countries.

The surname of those two enterprising brothers Andre and Edouard ....Michelin !

Michelin stars are awarded for excellence to a select few establishments. The acquisition or loss of a star can have dramatic effects on the success of a business. Become Michelin starred and produce excellence time after time!

83. And The Winner Is.....

Far from the eagerly anticipated and globally televised event it is today, the first Academy Awards ceremony took place out of the public eye during an Academy banquet at the Hollywood Roosevelt Hotel. Two hundred and seventy people attended the May 16, 1929 dinner in the hotel's Blossom Room; guest tickets cost $5. And there was little suspense when the awards were presented that night, as the recipients had already been announced three months earlier!

Since 2001, the Oscar ceremony has been held in Hollywood's Dolby Theatre and in 2014 the 86th Annual Academy Awards had a total viewership of 43.7 million. As a glamorous star of stage and screen strolls out to the podium, they briefly pause, before informing us of all the nominees for the particular category. We then view selected clips from each of their movies before the audience is hushed, the celebrity holds up and opens the envelope and announces: The winner is..............wait, hold up, stop there, in cinema terms re-wind.

Let's firstly ask; How do you get nominated? Into the final few, placed on that prized shortlist?
Lots of industries have one. As a young singer you may be sitting around the table with your manager chatting about your next song and someone suggests, "Maybe we could get Paulo Nutini to write it?"
Or the ad agency and the client are discussing the new campaign, and

inevitably, someone says, "Maybe Nigella Lawson could be our spokesperson...."
And Noel Edmunds to chair, Andy Murray to endorse, Duncan Bannatyne to invest, you get the idea.

In business often on the shortlist are the esteemed, obvious choices. The people who are seen as making it all come together.

So, how do YOU get on THAT shortlist? After all, once you are on the shortlist, not only do your fees double, but the amount of work increases to the point where you can't possibly do it all. Like we mentioned previously, it's easy to seduce yourself into thinking it's a straight up meritocracy. The funniest comedians, the most talented chefs, the most impactful speakers - these gifted individuals are chosen for the shortlist because they deserve it.
Except that is not correct.

Yes, of course, you need a minimum amount of talent to make the shortlist. It might even help to be a genius. But plenty of people with talent (and plenty of geniuses) aren't there, aren't thought of by industry outsiders and those looking for a straightforward way to bring on someone they can trust.

No, the shortlist requires more than that. Luck, sure, but also the persistence of doing the work in the right place in the right way for a very long time. Not an overnight success, but one that took a decade or three.

The secret of getting on the shortlist is doing your best work fearlessly for a long time before you get on the list, and (especially) doing it even if you are not on the list!

Glenn Close has been on the Oscar shortlist six times but has yet to win. In 2012, the Academy named Christopher Plummer, at age 82, as the Best Actor in a Supporting Role, he became the oldest winner in any acting category for his performance in Beginners. As he clutched his statuette, the debonaire thespian addressed it thus: "You're only two years older than me darling, where have you been all of my life?"

Plummer had been in the industry for over 60 years building his audience.

Trade the dream of overnight success for slow, measured growth. It can be hard, but you have to be patient, stick with it, you have to be willing to grind it out. You often have to do it for a long time before the right people notice. Again, once you have some customers and a history, you'll have a story to tell.

 *Just launching isn't a good story. Continue to get people interested in what you have to say, and then keep at it. In a few years, you will get to chuckle when people discuss your "overnight" success!*

84. The Nights...

"The Nights" is a song by Swedish DJ and music producer Avicii. It features uncredited vocals by American recording artist Nicholas "RAS" Furlong, who co-wrote the song with Jordan Suecof, Gabriel Benjamin, and John Feldmann.

Furlong noted that he began writing the song as an ode to his father. The inspiration for the sound came to him while at a bar in Ireland. Furlong recalls, "I had been going back and forth with Jordan and Gabe about this song idea that merged commercially sound rock music with the signature sound of an Irish drinking song. When I returned to Los Angeles we all went into the studio. As soon as Gabe began playing the guitar riff everything just sort of clicked." Furlong sent the original idea, titled "My Father Told Me", to Ash Pournouri, Avicii's manager.

Pournouri recognized an immediate draw to the track, saying that the song had that same sense of euphoria which characterizes so much of Avicii's music. In an interview with Yahoo Music, Pournouri said, "It made absolute sense to work on it with Ras," adding that he and Avicii just needed "to make it more 'us' and that's what [we] did."

Like his previous hits "Wake Me Up" and "Hey Brother, "The Nights" is a progressive house song containing elements of folk rock.

The official music video for "The Nights" was released onto YouTube December 15, 2014 and premiered on the front page of Yahoo Music. The video was produced, directed by, and stars "professional life liver" Rory Kramer, who filmed an exuberant action-packed recollection of his own life on roller coasters, surfing, snowboarding, skateboarding, balloon flying, etc.

Watch the video, be inspired and live a life to be remembered!

85. Hats Off To Business Success...

When was the last day you went shopping for a new hat?

They reckon the origin of the term milliner is probably the Middle English milener, meaning an inhabitant of the city of Milan. A milliner designs, makes, trims or sells hats. Millinery is the designing and manufacture of hats.

We can be asked to wear a multitude of different hats during the course of a working day. Often we're required to carry out a variety of roles: Ranging from hosting an early morning meeting, heading challenging discussions or planning important sales strategies. Possibly you're about to begin a new project, motivate others, write up monthly reports or deliver a vital team talk.

We need to have the ability to reappear, resurface and reinvent ourselves every minute of every day. Serving mini apprenticeships, receiving 24 hour degrees and putting on an array of outfits with helmets to match! A small example of the duties we may well be required to carry out as milliners and the character traits they empower us with, include some of the following:

Musician - amplify all that they stand for.

Vocalist - teaching the world to sing.

Chef - preparing their signature dish, specific to you and your brand.

Magician - creating magical Ta-Raa moments.

Clapperboard operator - able to reshoot, redo, retake, to seek out perfection.

Storyteller - creative, imaginative, enthralling and captivating.

Writer - like Dickens not average, good or mediocre, but GREAT EXPECTATIONS.

Executioner - the ability to follow up, to carry out and action.

Builder - can lay solid foundations, strengthen others.

Starter - take initiative, move forward, build momentum.

Mountain Climber - endure, steady, reliable, strive to peak & reach the summit.

Pioneer - believe in what they are doing, into unknown, break new ground.

Traveller - love diversity, what other cultures bring, seeker of knowledge.

Postman - no matter the difficult conditions he can be trusted to deliver.

Artist - starts with a blank canvas and precedes to produce masterpieces.

Cyclist - at ease in the slipstream, able to change gear improve, go faster, overtake.

Jockey - covers a lot of ground, capable sprinter and overcomes hurdles.

Lifeguard - patient, watches, protects, ultimate life saver.

Schoolteacher - can instill passion & curiosity, a tutor, a mentor, a role model.

Sherlock - magnify your abilities, a questioner, why, why why?

Prospector - determined, mining for gold, treasure and hidden gems.

What is the most interesting hat, cap or piece of imaginery headgear that you have ever been asked or required to wear? One that helped you address and solve a major issue, cost or concern.

Choose your hat carefully, small gestures can have an enormous impact. They have the power to change someone's day!

86. The Lion & The Unicorn...

It has been said that after meeting with legendary British Prime Minister William Gladstone, you left feeling he was the smartest person in the world, but after meeting with his rival Benjamin Disraeli, you left thinking YOU were the smartest person in the world.

Gladstone or Disraeli which one do you desire to be?

87. People...

Birds of a feather flock together

People like people who truly listen to them. People like people who flatter them and talk about their interests. People like people who remember their name.

People like people who show a real and genuine interest in them. People like people who are like them.

 Become a People Person!

88. Dyb, dyb, dyb - Do Your Best...

A certain kind of individual puts on that uniform: Trustworthy; Loyal; Helpful; Friendly; Kind; Courteous; Thrifty; Brave; Obedient; Cheerful; Clean and Reverent.

 Be that individual!

89. A Pathfinder...

...the Scouting motto since 1907 allows you to embrace all of the following:

Adapt - Coach - Equip - Develop - Adjust - Contrive - Anticipate - Fabricate - Build up - Cook - Appoint - Fashion - Dispose - Fix - Arrange - Brace - Form - Make - Lay the groundwork - Plan - Draw up - Perfect - Assemble - Fit out - Concoct - Produce - Fill in - Put together - Construct - Formulate - Provide - Fortify - Practice - Gird - Make provision - Furnish - Put in order - Qualify - Ready - Settle - Train - Steel - Outfit - Groom - Make up - Turn out - Prime - Smooth the way - Supply - Strengthen - Warm up.

Be prepared to find your own path!

90. Toffee Bob, an Inspiring Story...

The history of Toffee Bob unwraps the sweet and surprising life story of one of Scotland's best-known retailers.

Unlike his two fellow retailing legends of the High Street, W H Smith and John

Menzies, there was always more to R S McColl than an ability to sell confectionery over the counter in the many newsagents' shops which continue to bear his well-kent name.

In fact, Robert Smyth McColl can justly lay claim to having been Scotland's first soccer superstar. Not that the man himself would have boasted about his prowess as a footballer. So much so, in fact, that many Scots are entirely unaware that R S McColl was ever anything other than the brand-name above the doors of a nationwide chain of sweetie vendors.

In fact, within the space of 13 months he succeeded in scoring three hat-tricks against each of the other home countries. If he'd played in the current era, McColl would undoubtedly be hailed as a global superstar, he'd certainly be rated in the £ 25-30m transfer fee bracket. McColl had his greatest days as an amateur with Queen's Park in Glasgow.

He did make some money, but it wasn't until he turned professional in 1901 with

Newcastle United that he began his path to financial achievement. When McColl did finally head south, he was similarly shrewd about which club he chose - and just as canny in what he opted to do with his signing-on fee. He went to Newcastle because they were offering him a pound a week more than Liverpool - £ 5 per week. They also gave him £ 300, which was a sizeable sum in 1901. He obviously figured the big money wouldn't last forever and so chose to invest £ 100 of it with his brother, Tom, who had a sweet-manufacturing business and three shops under the T N McColl name. Bob's money led the pair to expand the firm - and the shops name changed to R S McColl, cashing in on Bob's football celebrity.

Cinema was the booming social novelty of the day all over Scotland at this time, and Bob McColl apparently derived great joy from finding prime locations for his sweetie shops - many of them next door to cinemas. By the time of the Wall Street Crash in 1929, the McColl brothers had 150 shops. R S McColl was sold to Cadbury's in 1931, although the day-to-day running of the business remained in the hands of Bob and Tom. From that day onwards, the McColls were both wealthy men.

If he came across worthy employees in other newsagent-confectioners, he'd give them jobs with his firm. When a pal became unemployed, he once bought a cinema for him to manage. More to the point, McColl always re-united his Scotland team mates from the momentous 1900 victory over England in order to take them down to the game at Wembley every other year for an all-expenses-paid treat.

Unfortunately, McColl's English playing career wasn't a happy one. Anglo cloggers kept crocking him. He returned to Glasgow to play for Rangers briefly, before being accepted back into the purer-than-pure ranks of amateurism by the noble chaps of Queen's Park. In his last home game for Queen's Park in 1910, R S McColl scored six goals in a league game against Port Glasgow. Over a century later that remains the greatest goal-scoring feat that has ever been accomplished in a single game at Hampden.

During an international career which spanned the years from 1896 to 1908, R S McColl gained 13 Scottish caps, all of them against the three home nations, England, Wales, and Northern Ireland. During all that time, McColl only ever finished on the losing side on one occasion. He managed a commendable tally of 13 goals in his 13 Scotland appearances - nine of these goals being scored in three games.

Operated by McColls Retail Group, there are currently around 200 Scottish branches of R S McColl.

Learn to develop skills in more than one area, look to the future and secure your legacy!

91. Competition...

Author Roland Huntford wrote Scott & Amundsen: The Last Place on Earth. It was a sensation when it first appeared in the late seventies. Many years later I still find it an engrossing and instructive narrative, with vivid characterisation and a mass of useful detail.

When you finish it you know much more about human nature, for it is more than a book about the South Pole. It is about two leaders, two cultures, and about the nature of exploration itself, which is to me a counterpart to the creative impulse, requiring mental toughness, imagination, courage, and a leap of faith.

He examined every detail of the great race to the South Pole between Britain's Robert Scott and Norway's Roald Amundsen. Scott, who died along with four of his men, became Britain's beloved failure, while Amundsen, who not only beat Scott but returned alive, was largely forgotten.

Gripping and highly readable, 'The Last Place on Earth' captures the driving ambitions of the era and the complex, often deeply flawed men who were charged with carrying them out.

Most of all, this book about a race, which was the last great expedition that ended the Age of Discovery, is a study in leadership.

92. Innovative...

True leaders in any field go beyond the norm to break new ground through innovation. They become the example of what is possible, and they are always changing the game in positive ways.

Be an innovative individual, exemplify remarkable performance; set new standards of excellence in all that you do and lead an inspired life.

93. Float Like a Butterfly...

What did Muhammad Ali say before he was world champion? 'I am the greatest.'
What did he say when he was the greatest? 'I am the greatest.'

What does he say now when he's no longer the greatest? 'I am the greatest.'

 The perfect affirmation.

94. Everlasting Gaffes...

In the early days of the struggle to dominate the soft-drinks market the Coca-Cola Company were offered the chance to acquire the small firm of Pepsi-Cola, which had twice been bankrupt, for just $1000.

However, since Coca-Cola controlled all but a small share of the market at that time the board did not feel inclined to waste $1000 on a company which was likely to disappear soon in any event. After all, they reasoned, how many people would be drinking Pepsi-Cola in the future?

Learn from our mistakes; We may be products of our past, but as Penalty Takers we don't have to be prisoners to it!

95. Start Up...

"The starting point of all achievement is desire.
Without continual growth and progress, such words as improvement, achievement and success have no meaning. Make the most of yourself by fanning the tiny, inner sparks of possibility into flames of achievement."

- Napoleon Hill, Benjamin Franklin, Golda Meir.

Strike the match, take the first step and continue to endure and to summit!

96. One Giant Leap...

Do you think of yourself as extraordinary? Are you rolling your eyes because you think extraordinary is some special, unattainable status held by a privileged few?

Becoming extraordinary rarely hinges on what you can or can't do. More often it lies in what you will or won't do.

As author Mark Sanborn wrote on his blog, "Every morning when we wake up, we are confronted with a choice: another day just like the last or a clean slate to start all over."

Make today the day you choose to pursue an extraordinary life!

97. The Question is...

Coach Marshall Goldsmith, Ph.D., learned this exercise from his daughter, Kelly Goldsmith, Ph, D., who was on the marketing faculty of the Kellogg School of Management at Northwestern University. It's built around the "one question in life you can't blame on somebody else:
Did I do my best?

That's one thing you can control," Marshall Goldsmith says. Ask yourself the following questions every day to stay on track toward goals and focus on the things in your life that are within your control.
Did I do my best to:

* Set clear goals?
* Make progress toward goal achievement?
* Be happy?
* Find Meaning?
* Build positive relationships?
* Be fully engaged?

This self-coaching technique has proved to be highly effective, according to 79 unpublished (as of press time) studies of more than 2,500 people. The research found that for those who repeated the six-question process daily for two weeks, 37 percent responded that they were improving on all six points; 65 percent responded that they were improving on at least four of six; and 88 percent responded that they were improving on at least one.

With daily commitment comes long term solutions!

98. Winners Never Cheat...

You may not have heard of Jon Huntsman, but the people he has assisted over the years sure have. Ask the people of Armenia. Now there's a story worth telling.

On the evening of December 7, 1988, Jon and Karen Huntsman were watching the news in the living room of their striking Salt Lake City home. He was CEO and chairman of Huntsman Chemical Corporation - an upstart in the stodgy and traditional chemical industry.

The lead story on the nightly news was unsettling: An earthquake had devastated much of Armenia. Jon was riveted by the scenes of destruction unfolding before him: factories and apartments in rubble, roads and railways little more than twisted pretzels of concrete and steel, school buildings flattened, frantic survivors clawing through debris for loved ones.

A year earlier, Jon Huntsman probably could not have located Armenia on the map, but in the six previous months he had negotiated with Aeroflot, the airline of the old Soviet government, to manufacture in a new Moscow plant plastic service ware for in-flight meals. In the process, he became the first American permitted to own a majority interest in a Soviet business. He had become fascinated with the USSR bear, and now disaster had struck one of its satellite states.

"We have to do something," he said to Karen that night. He was taking the suffering before him personally.

The aid that followed ranged from expertise and resources for a modern cement factory that would produce concrete that could withstand most quakes to food and medical equipment to apartment complexes and schools - all as gifts to a grateful, battered nation.

Before he was finished 15 years later, the Huntsman family had infused $50 million of its money into Armenia, visiting the nation two dozen times. Yet, on that December 1988 night, he had no ties to that region of the world. He didn't know the name of a single victim. But the name Huntsman is not unknown in Armenia today, where Jon is an honorary citizen and recipient of the nation's highest award.

Who is Jon Huntsman? Ask those who have been helped. Ask the communities around the globe where Huntsman Corp. does business. They will tell of the deep, personal interest he has in their fortunes, their families, and their futures.

📖 *As you look to succeed in life, learn to train your eyes on the possibilities, not the odds. That you are motivated not solely on profits and power, but also on making a difference in the lives of others.*

99. Make Them Listen...

"The argument which is made by a man's life is more weight than that which is furnished by words." ISOCRATE

📖 *People will sit up and listen, when they see you in action!*

100. Smile, say Cheese...

Having the market's attention is not enough to guarantee success. According to Brian Solis, just seventy-one companies from the original *Fortune* 500 compiled in 1955 remain on the list today, and generations of families capturing "Kodak moments" on film couldn't save Kodak from its downward spiral. The company filed for Chapter 11 bankruptcy in 2012. That same year, the four person team who built the photo sharing app Instagram, and gave their product away to millions of people for free, was acquired by Facebook for a record-breaking billion dollars. Everything we knew about brand equity, it seemed, had finally turned on its head.

Real marketing is built into what you do and why you do it.

101. Be Important...

Products can be similar, but missions are unique. You don't want people to buy your stuff; you want to matter to them. You want them to care about your brand.

To believe in what you do. To 'buy in.' Part of your mission is to get those people, not everyone, but the ones you care about, to care.

The mission of an artist isn't to sell her stuff to the masses; it's to sell the ideas conveyed in those things, maybe to just 1000 true fans. The artist buys into the idea that she not only expresses herself through her art, but also helps others to do the same. Her mission is to shape culture, to communicate beauty, stimulate thought and make an emotional connection.

Your product might be similar, but your mission is unique. All you have to do is turn up the volume by amplifying your difference and telling a better story than the competition.

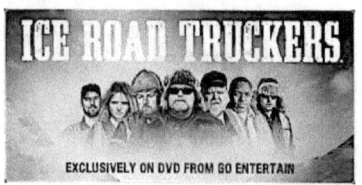

102. Behind the Scenes...

Give people a backstage pass and show them how your business works. Imagine that someone wanted to make a reality show about your business. What would they share? Now stop waiting for someone else and do it yourself.

Think no one will care? Think again. Even seemingly boring jobs can be fascinating when presented right. What could be more boring than commercial fishing and trucking? Yet the Discovery Channel and History Channel have turned these professions into highly rated shows: Deadliest Catch and Ice Road Truckers.

Let people behind the curtain and change your relationship with them. They'll develop a deeper level of understanding and appreciation for what you do.

103. Half Empty or Half Full?

We can argue forever about the merits of being an optimist or a pessimist.

Ultimately, however, the contents of the glass don't matter; what's more important is to realize there is a jug of water nearby. In other words, we have the capacity to refill the glass, or to change our outlook. I would say that the world itself is the container. Life is the jug. Begin building your positive outlook by asking yourself these questions:

 *How can I reach out and better connect with my co-workers, neighbours or friends? What are some ways my actions matter to the world? What am I proud of accomplishing today?*

104. Gathering Momentum...

Perhaps you wouldn't be surprised to know that a locomotive traveling 55 mph could crash right through a 5-foot-thick steel-reinforced concrete wall without stopping. But do you realize that the same train, starting from a stationary position, wouldn't be able to roll over an inch-thick block placed in front of its driving wheel? There's an important lesson here that applies to your work as a leader: The size of your problem generally isn't your problem. Instead it's a lack of momentum that's stalling you at the train yard. Without momentum, even the smallest obstacle can prevent you from moving forward. But with it you can plow through anything.

Remove barriers now, so that you and your team can experience marvelous, incredible breakthroughs, that are richly deserved!

105. Night After Night...

Whenever actor Liam Neeson and his late wife Natasha Richardson did theatre, they kept a Samuel Beckett quote in their dressing room as inspiration. "You've come offstage," Neeson says, "you've done a lousy performance for whatever reason, and you get a chance to go on stage the next night and the night after that for four or five months. You make it better, but you have to come back to the plate again. You have to keep always coming back to the plate."

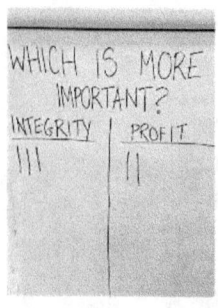 *"Ever tried. Ever failed. No matter. Try again. Fail Again. Fail better."*
- Samuel Beckett

106. More Integrity, More Profits...

Author Tony Simon argues that integrity affects the bottom line. Simons, a Cornell University professor and sales management consultant, drew that conclusion after surveying more than 6,800 employees at 76 hotels (all of them franchises of one hotel chain). He found that small differences in employees' perceptions of whether their managers live by their word - by integrity - translated into large differences in that hotel's profitability.

These differences were measurable and significant for the average employee of a single hotel: Just a quarter of a point on the 10-point scale was equal to about $250,000 a year, or 2.5 percent of revenues at one of the hotels. Simons dubbed this effect "The Integrity Dividend."

Lead by the power of your word!

107. Post a Demand Notice...

In November 1993, toy tycoon Ty Warner introduced Beanie Babies at the Smoky Mountain Gift Show in Gatlinburg, Tenn. "Always prepared to build hype, Warner had only two of the Beanies available for sale at the event," writes Zac Bissonnette.

"Seven more were on display but not then available for order." Implying or creating a shortage by "retiring" certain Beanie Babies was a tactic Warner employed repeatedly to ratchet up demand. Eventually his scheme worked. By the mid-1990's, "the children's toy transitioned to an adult obsession."

Warner had orchestrated a craze that swept the country with the help of some Beanie Baby-obsessed Illinois housewives (at the height of the craze in 1998, a single Beanie Baby sold for $10,000). Warner made a fortune and thrived until the Internal Revenue Service caught up with him.

In 2013 he pleaded guilty in a huge offshore tax-evasion case. Bissonnette has penned a mesmerizing tale about speculative collectibles, personal demons, love affairs, greed and gullibility.

Create what people love before they know they want it!

108. Watch This Space...

I was at a meeting recently and heard a fascinating story.

I was speaking to a highly successful property developer and he was telling me about a startling experience he had in Paris. He loves watches and decided to visit the main store of Patek Phillipe, the eminent watch maker.

As you'd expect, there was a extensive array of watches, most priced around the five to ten thousand pound mark.

Then suddenly he saw something that stopped him in his tracks.

There, glistening in a glass case was a watch with a price tag of one million dollars.

I kid you not, they sell a million dollar watch.

But even more amazing was this: he said in order to buy this watch you must write to the CEO of Patek Phillipe and tell him why you deserve it!

Can you believe that? They have the gall to charge a million for a watch and then you have to pass a test to see if you are worthy of it? Amazing.

And brilliant marketing.
By making you apply to buy the watch they change their position in the sales relationship. They move from someone hoping for a sale to someone in charge. They also make the watch seem even more desirable – it is for those who are exemplary in not one but two ways: They are extremely financially successful and also a true connoisseur of time pieces. They also dramatically reduce the chances of the buyer asking for a discount. The buyer is just hoping to be accepted.

Furthermore, and very importantly, even if they never sell this watch, they have positioned ALL of the other watches in the store as good value by comparison.
And positioned Patek Phillipe even more strongly at the top of the brand exclusivity ladder.
Wow. That is truly great marketing.

Now I'm not of course suggesting that you charge a million dollars for your product (unless you feel you can get away with it of course).

But I do ask you to have a think about how you could do something similar.

Consider how you could both create a premium priced product and make people fill out an application to buy it.

Make them prove they are worthy of your product, make it seem only for a select few, the deserving handful who appreciate it's extraordinary value.

It may seem paradoxical, but making it hard to buy a product very often increases the customer's desire for it.

We all want what we can't have.

Conversely, if you look too eager to sell something, the customer usually doesn't want to buy it.

Masters of business are very aware of this conundrum and therefore think very carefully about both their pricing and the availability of their goods (i.e. Beanie Babies).They don't just sell. They make people want to buy.

109.
Focus on
Today...

> The saddest fact I know is that most people have forgotten the fact that there is a genius inside them and they can do remarkable things with their life, whether they work as a street sweeper or running a company."
>
> ~ Robin Sharma

One of my favourite sayings is, "Yesterday ended last night." It doesn't matter whether yesterday was good or bad. It's over. Don't get stuck there. For that matter, don't think too much about the future, either. You can't change the past; you can't mold the future. But you can influence what happens right now.

Give the present day your full attention and best effort. Someone has to be the best. Why not you?

110. Be a Thinker...

Henry Ford, the great automotive genius, learned of a process for turning wood scraps from the production of Model T's into charcoal briquets.

He built a charcoal plant and Ford Charcoal was created (later renamed Kingsford Charcoal).

Today, Kingsford is still the leading manufacturer of charcoal in America. Catering consultancy companies don't usually think about writing books. Bands don't usually think about filming the recording process, and car manufacturers don't usually think about selling charcoal!

Without doubt, there is probably something you haven't thought about that you could sell too. What is it?

111. Decisions, Decisions...

When you put off decisions, they pile up. Piles then end up ignored, dealt with in haste or thrown out. As a result, the individual problems in those piles stay un-resolved.

Whenever you can, swap "Let's think about it" for " Let's decide on it". Commit to making decisions. Don't wait for the perfect solution, decide and move forward.

You want to get into the rhythm of making choices. When you get in that flow of making decision after decision, you build momentum and boost morale.
Decisions are progress. Each one you make is a brick in your foundation. You cannot build on top of "We'll decide later", but you can decorate and build on top of "Done".

Long projects zap morale. The longer it takes to develop, the less likely it is to launch. Make the call, make progress and get something out now - while you've got the motivation and momentum to do so!

112. Wow! I didn't Expect that...

When was the last time you surprised or delighted a customer, colleague or boss?

If you did, would it help?

Apple developed a tradition of secrecy largely because Steve Jobs saw the extraordinary value in surprising the audience. It creates a rare wave of excitement - remarkable is a byproduct of surprise. Today, they continue to work at the secrecy, as if that's the only element necessary to create surprise.

But of course, it's not.

Surprise comes from defying expectations. Sometimes, we have the negative surprises that come from missing those expectations, but in fact, those negative surprises are part of the process of exceeding them... if you're not prepared to live with a disappointment, you can't be in the business of seeking delight.

(The above was a blog by Seth Godin, an extraordinary man who continues to surprise and delight at every turn)

Effort matters, sure, but mostly surprise comes from caring enough about your audience that you're willing to fail in your effort to redefine what they expect from you. The vulnerability and intimacy that come from that leap are at the heart of what people talk about.

113. Believe It and Live It...

When you don't know what you believe, everything becomes an argument. Everything is debatable. But when you stand for something, decisions are obvious.

An excellent example of this in recent years is Vinnie's well known Sub Shop in downtown Chicago. They put this homemade basil oil on subs that's just perfect. You had better show up on time though. Ask when they close and the woman behind the counter will respond, "We close when the bread runs out." Really? "Yeah, we get our bread from the bakery down the street early in the morning, when it's freshest. Once we run out (usually around two or three p.m.), we close up shop. We could get more bread later in the day, but it's not as good as fresh baked bread in the morning. There's no point selling a few more sandwiches if the bread isn't good. A few bucks isn't going to make up for selling food we can't be proud of."

 *What do you offer or supply that you are proud of?*
Wouldn't you rather eat at Vinnie's instead of some generic sandwich chain?
Standing for something isn't just about writing it down.
It is about believing it and living it!

114. A Healthy Slice of Productivity...

It's easy to put your head down and just work on what you think needs to be done. It's a lot harder to pull your head up and ask why?
Here are some important questions to ask yourself to ensure you're doing work that matters:
Why are you doing this?
What problem are you solving?
Is this actually useful?
Are you adding value?

Will this change behaviour?
Is there an easier way?
What could you be doing instead?
Is it really worth it?

Keep asking yourself (and others) the questions listed. You don't need to make it a formal process, but don't let it slide either. Also, don't be timid about your conclusions. Sometimes abandoning what you're working on is also the right move, even if you've already put in a lot of effort. Don't throw good time after bad work.

 *Pour yourself into your product and everything around your product too: how you sell it, how you support it, how you explain it, and how you deliver it. Competitors can never copy the 'YOU' in your product!*

115. Museum Magic...

It's the stuff
you leave out that matters. So constantly look for things to remove, simplify and

streamline. Be a curator. You don't make a great museum by putting all the art in the world into a single room. *That's a warehouse!*

What makes a museum great is the stuff that's not on the walls. Someone says NO! There is an editing process, a curator is involved.

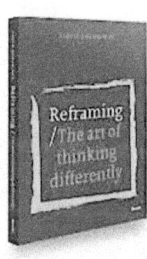 *Be that curator today, make conscious decisions about what should stay and what should go.*

116. The Art of Thinking Differently...

Think great thoughts and you're way more likely to lead a great life; it really is that simple if sometimes difficult to actually implement. As the great William James (American philosopher and psychologist) once said, "The greatest breakthrough in my lifetime is the realisation that man can alter his life by altering his thinking. We have approx. 70,000 thoughts per day, although many will be the same ones looping around and around. That is why we know that the quality of our thoughts is highly correlated to the quality of our life.

Consider reframing regularly - a reframe is where you decide to look at a negative situation in a more empowering light. It doesn't involve changing the actual event (that would be delusional), just adjusting your view of it.

Become good at reframing by simply asking yourself the following questions when things are not going to plan.
1.What else can this mean?
2. What can I learn from this?

117. The Power of Awe...

Awe is the sense of wonder and amazement that occurs when someone is inspired by great knowledge, beauty, sublimely or might.

It's the experience of confronting something greater than yourself. Awe expands ones frame of reference and drives self transcendence. It encompasses admiration and inspiration and can be evolved by everything from great works of art or music, to religious transformation. From breath taking natural landscapes, to human feats of daring and discovery. Awe is a complex emotion and frequently involves a sense of surprise, mystery and unexpectedness.

Check out some recent blog posts that have went viral. No matter what they involve, they will normally ALWAYS involve awe!

118. Mouth Watering Tips...

You are more likely to tip a waiter or waitress more if it's a sunny day, because the chemicals released in your brain put you in a more genial and generous frame of mind. Having said that, the effect of this if you live in a really hot country where sunshine is the norm is minimised.

Speaking of tipping, you are a lot more likely to increase your gratuity to a waiter who has gently touched your arm as you were ordering. You may not have even noticed the touch, but your brain has and it has equated that touch with friendship and familiarity.

'Thank you very much. Have a nice day!'

119. Mouth Watering Tips 2...

Regarding ordering your food. Did you know... you're 40 - 60% more likely to buy food you can reach out and touch than food somebody describes to you or places behind a counter. The old fashioned sweet trolleys really do generate more sales and top restaurants know this. In addition, did you know... your brain associates elaborate words and descriptions with higher prices. Therefore it is happier for you to pay more for crisps (potato chips) described as being "dusted in cracked black pepper and dipped in sea salt," than it would be for plain old salted crisps.

Almost unbelievably the same goes for fancy fonts in fancy restaurants that charge fancy prices. Spot an old English type of font and you'd better prepare yourself because you are being subtly guided to pay more than you may have expected.

Get yourself a copy of - How to Persuade and Influence People: Powerful Techniques to Get Your Own Way More Often by Philip Hesketh.

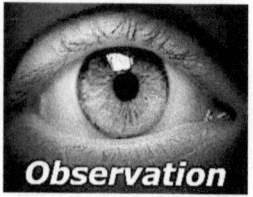
Observation

120. Watch and Learn...

The internet is awash with amateur psychology tips, from ludicrous life-affirming self-help ("Greet your alarm clock every morning by pumping your fist and shouting 'YEAH!'") to beginner level hypnotherapy disguised as creepy 'dating' tips, most of which you can (and should) safely ignore.

At the same time, there are some basic psychological and sociological truths that not only make sense, but you realize you've known all along.

In the absence of any sort of relevant qualification, here are some observations I've learned to trust over the years, that should help you work, rest and play with more confidence.

1. During an introduction, make a note of someone's eye colour. You're not going to use the information (unless you plan to write them a poem) – it's just a technique to achieve the optimum amount of eye

contact, which people find friendly and confident.

2. People always have the clearest memory of first and last thing that happens, while the middle becomes a vague blur. So if you're setting the time for an interview, try and be the first or last through the door.

3. People's feet are often an insight into what they're thinking. For example, if you approach two people talking and they turn their torso to you but not their feet, they'd prefer you left them alone. Similarly if you're talking to someone and their feet are pointing away from you, they want to escape.

4. Like all therapists worth their fee, remember to use the power of silence. If someone gives you an unsatisfactory answer to a question, stay quiet and keep eye contact and they'll usually feel pressured to keep talking and reveal more.

5. If you know someone is going to have a go at you in a meeting, deliberately sit right next to them. The proximity will make

them feel less comfortable with being aggressive, and you'll have an easier time of it.

6. Asking people for small favours trains their brain to believe they like you.

7. Difficult though it is, if you can get into the habit of not only remembering someone's name when you first meet them, but using their name in the subsequent conversation you have, they'll find you terribly charming and wonderful.

8. Mirroring people's body language when you interact with them is a way of building up trust. Just be subtle about it.

9. The best way to learn, is to teach. If you're acquiring a new skill or piece of knowledge, bore someone else with it at the first opportunity you get.

10. Finally: there is nothing more important to people than their self-image. Figure out how people like to think of themselves, and challenge or reinforce it to your advantage.

Anthropology is divided ordinarily and with reason into Anatomy, which considers the body and the parts, and Psychology, which speaks of the soul. Learn how to speak to the soul!

121. I Never Got It...

I must begin revision.
I must begin revision.
I must begin revision.

As a schoolboy in High School I never got it. Classrooms, timetables, teachers...nope! Homework, exams, foreign language...sorry! English, mathematics and science...whatever! I just never got it.

I DO NOW!

Life is a revision. Every minute, of every hour, of every day. Go study it!

122. Gearing for Growth...

"Tell me and I forget, teach me and I may remember, involve me and I learn" – *Benjamin Franklin*

Why do we spend so much of our time as leaders telling other people what to do and how to do things and then wonder why we don't have a team who can be innovative, provide solutions, work autonomously and take ownership?

As leaders is one of our greatest roles not to inspire, develop, encourage and challenge our teams to become the best they can be, to encourage them to continue to develop and learn and give them the space to take responsibility, deliver outcomes and take some calculated risks?

What impact would allowing your team members to be able to lead a project have on developing their skills? As the business leader do you need to be the leader of all your team need to deliver?

It often helps to put ourselves in the shoes of others and to remember what it felt like when we were given the freedom to make decisions and take risks knowing what we had to deliver and excited by the prospect of doing so or of over achieving.

Why is it that as children all we do is ask, but as adults all we often do is tell?

 *(The above were some stirring words from my friend Kirsty Bathgate, who is the founder of Gearing for Growth who work with growing businesses and leaders to support them to perform at their best, with less stress, better returns and more time for the important things in life.)*

123. As Young As You Feel...

The body may grow old, but the spirit never has to wrinkle. You'll lose plenty in life - people, energy and eventually independence, novelist Isabel Allende told a TED 2014 audience. But along the way you'll gain the freedom of self-confidence, among other treasures.

Allende's eight minute talk - now viewable for free at TED.com - explains how you can age gleefully, too.

The inspiring and reassuring talk is sure to spread a smile across your face, whatever your age.

The primary point? Retain your youthful mind.

124. The Rubik Cube of Social Media...

As more small businesses take to Facebook to promote themselves, many have seen a decline in the number of fans their posts actually reach. Yet a study by social media marketing company Komfo found that engagement rates are actually increasing.

Komfo's study analysing over 8,000 business pages worldwide from August 2013 to August 2014 discovered the reach of those pages dropped from 25.2 percent to 11.34 percent over the course of the year. But the click - through rate increased from 5.62 percent to 8.32 percent.

What does this mean for your business page? Your post may not reach 100,000 people - it might not even reach 1,000 people - but the people it does reach will interact with the post.

Create better content that engages your fans to maintain your engagement rates!

125. Not Just a Numbers Game...

Following on from the Social Media post and with regards to creating better content that engages with people, I thought I would follow it up with three key ways to achieve it:

1. Get Feedback - Worried your new product won't do well? Use Facebook to predict its success. Ask your audience for opinions about your new products. Your loyal fans will share their thoughts. Questions like these will help increase engagement and make them feel valuable as customers.

2. Invoke Emotion - A study by the online content analysis tool BuzzSumo examined 100 million articles to find out what makes content go viral. It found articles that invoked awe, laughter and amusement were most successful. Rather than posting something possibly informative but dull about your product or service, try posting something funny that will make your audience laugh.

3. Use Visuals - Don't just share links to articles or boring text: get creative and share images. The same study by BuzzSumo found that when a post included an image, it was twice as likely to be shared.

Message; Share; Like; Comment; Add Friend; Photos & Follow!

126. Ready, Aim, Fire...

I once heard the late Zig Ziglar tell an audience that he could teach each person in that room to beat the world's top archer. He followed up by stating all he'd need to do is line them all up, show them how to pull back the bow and aim at their targets. And then he would blindfold the Olympic champ!

Zig's point is well taken: Even a stellar performer can't hit his target unless he knows where to aim.

In sales, most people are content with a squishy goal such as "I want my sales to be better than last year's." But everyone wants his or her numbers to be better than last year's, and that isn't a specific enough target. "Better" doesn't allow you to build the plans to ensure that you grow your sales number or be certain that you succeeded.

Specify your number, set your target. Then work backward to accurately map your sales plan!

127. The Week Ahead...

GUESS WHAT? YOU HAVE A BRAND NEW WEEK AHEAD OF YOU TO SLAY DRAGONS, ACHIEVE GOALS, SWEAT MORE, GRIPE LESS AND DITCH THE FEAR! GO!

Monday: Grant me the strength to focus this week, to be mindful and present, to serve with excellence, to be loving and good natured.

Tuesday: Do not delay difficult decisions or avoid new habits necessary to advance your life. What must be done should be done with haste, for life is precious.

Wednesday: When you are alive with joy, gratitude and genuine interest in others, you are at your most beautiful.

Thursday: No blaming. What defines us is not our past but the vision, discipline, resilience and heart we bring to this very day.

Friday: Today is the gateway to your weekend. Don't be lazy or play at half-speed.

Being excellent today allows freedom tomorrow. Now go stun the world!

128. Setting a Course...

Ranked the most popular leadership and management expert in the world by Inc. in 2014, John C. Maxwell says:
"There's no question that everything I am today is because I decided to grow every day of my life. We cannot go any further than our growth. In the 1970s, my friend Curt Kampmeir asked me what my personal growth plan was. I had none.

He said to me, "Growth is not an automatic process." That was life-changing. He set me on a course of intentional living.

I came to the conclusion that four things would make a person successful: relationships, attitude, the ability to train and equip people, and the ability to lead. I decided to grow in these areas. I also realised I needed to to grow my strengths: connecting and communicating with people.

I had these essentials that I would grow in, and then I purposely began to interview people who had these strengths. I began to read books about these subjects and to focus on things that would bring a high return in my personal growth. I do that every day.

When I meet people, I ask questions to help me learn: Are there people you know whom I should know? What book have you read that I should read? Where have you been that I ought to go myself?"

Anyone who wants to continue learning daily must be intentional. They have to set aside time. They have to make it a priority!

129. A Winning Quality...

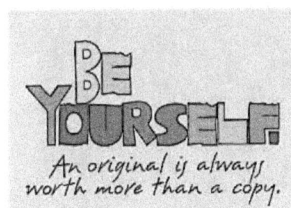

An original is always worth more than a copy.

It's easy to get squeezed into what others want you to do. You have to search your own heart, be willing to say no and be willing to disappoint some people - because you're not going to please yourself if you're not true to yourself.

When you go out expecting people to like you, expecting to be at the right place at the right time, that's going to open up the door for good things to come into your life.

You'll never reach your highest potential if you have limited expectations. If you are still at the same place you were five years ago, you are falling behind.

You should be learning something every day. Every person and situation in your life are there to teach you something. Stay open to change!

130. Don't Be a Spectator...

In his 2014 autobiography 'The Second Half,' Roy Keane, the ex-Manchester Utd and Forest star, talked openly about an important European tie played in Portugal. FC Porto managed at the time by Jose Mourinho were the first leg opponents when Keane was sent off in that match, thus missing the return game at Old Trafford two weeks later.

Keane, watching from the stand thought to himself - "If I had been playing it could have been different."

His exact quote was, "I hated being a spectator, it was horrible. The result might have been different if I had been playing."

Every player should feel that. You have to feel that you can make a difference!

131. 'Keane' to Follow Up...

A second quote from the Roy Keane autobiography talks about when he briefly played for Celtic Football Club near the end of his career. It allowed him the opportunity to meet kitman, John Clark, who had been part of the 1967 'Lisbon Lions' European Cup winning team, and now was an invaluable member of the backroom staff at Celtic Park.

In Roys own words he states:

"The kit man is vital, he is almost the hub of everything, a link to everybody. He has to be good humoured and upbeat. You have to be glad to see the kit man in the morning, he reflects everything about the club in a sense."

In business as in life, it is vital we have people around us that smooth the way, that keep us motivated, understand us and put a reassuring arm around us from time to time. Do you treasure and value your kit man?

132. I'll Be Back...

As the Planet Hollywood brand developed and grew in the early days, spreading their message was essential, creating an awareness was vitally important as new locations were opening up around the world.

Before 'instant' social media, texts, tweets and snapchat, people were still able to generate an excitement and a desire to be involved, to be in attendance, to 'turn up.'

When they opened in Moscow, ten thousand people turned up. Then in London that number increased to over forty thousand. Their opening in San Antonio, Texas, turned into a citywide celebration where more than one hundred thousand people were partying in the streets. It was a huge sensation. There was no press that didn't cover the openings.

In the words of Arnold Schwarzenegger: "Planet Hollywood was like the Beatles: a genius idea with sophisticated promotion and the best marketing."

Get the buzz out there for your project, business or service. Create your very own "Planet Hollywood!'

133. Open Sesame...

When you think of Alibaba, you probably think of an Arabian folk tale involving 40 thieves and a hidden den of treasure.

These days though, Alibaba is much more than a legendary folklore figure. Alibaba is one of the world's biggest e-commerce companies, even though most people in the world have never heard of them.

Despite the distinctly Arabian sounding name, Alibaba is a Chinese company.

It is an online marketplace that is actually bigger than, wait for it...both Amazon and Ebay COMBINED!

It is estimated that 80% of online sales in China - the world's second largest economy - go through Alibaba and the array of companies it owns. When Jack Ma was born back in 1964, China was a remarkably different place.

The best way to understand Alibaba is as a mix of Amazon.com, eBay and PayPal with a dash of Google thrown in, all with some uniquely Chinese characteristics. Alibaba plays a middleman role, which is where the eBay comparisons come in. However, there is no bidding, which is where the Amazon comparisons come in. Because it makes money off of ad revenues, Google comparisons are thrown in the mix.

Jack Ma founded Alibaba in 1999. It is an amazing rags-to-riches story. He's a small guy, barely five feet tall. He is not imposing and is affectionately known as "Crazy Jack Ma'.

From starting with nothing, his net worth today according to the Bloomberg Billionaires index is estimated at over $21 billion. The story of his rise to wealth and power is both fascinating and inspiring.

"When you hear the sound of the starting gun, you don't look around and see how your opponents are doing. You just run like crazy!"
Jack Ma (Executive Chairman of Alibaba)

134. Stance, Viewpoint, Position...

To be persuasive we must be believable. To be believable we must be credible. To be credible we must be truthful. Ability is what you're capable of doing. Motivation determines what you do. Attitude determines how well you do it!

If someone likes you, they'll buy what you're selling whether they need it or not.

135. Be Part of Something Bigger...

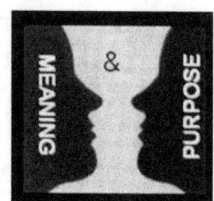

People who have meaning and purpose in their lives are happier, feel more in control and get more out of what they do. They also experience less stress, anxiety and depression. But where do we find "meaning and purpose"? It might be our religious faith, being a parent or doing a job that makes a difference. The answers vary for each of us, but they all involve being connected to something bigger than ourselves.

 Give your life meaning and purpose!

136. Say Cheese...

Become a photographer, like a photograph you develop from negatives.

So, go shoot the family, hang the kids and frame the wife!

 *Smile, invite people in, give them a snapshot of your life and keep your image intact!*

137. Stops, Mishaps and Detours...

Sometimes we see signs that say or illustrate a dead end or a one way street. In life, we should avoid those options that ultimately corral us into a place where our choices are limited, we feel under pressure to agree or to go along with the crowd. Get yourself in a place with large roundabouts and a variety of exit options. Roads that will get you to your final destination, complete with stops, mishaps and detours. Some longer, some shorter, but still on course. Even when you go off the beaten track and your car runs out of fuel, you know what, have humility, reach out to others, bless their lives by allowing them to help you!

My wife and I picked up a hitchhiker recently on our 2014 wedding anniversary. It was a short distance between Clydebank and Dumbarton, in the West of Scotland. He was going further North to Fort William and I would have willingly taken him to his final destination because his stories in our brief ten minutes where amazing! He confided in us, total strangers! Hopefully, you can place your trust in others, let them help, assist and offer support. Go humbly thumb a lift, recognise the power of acceptance, stop resisting and find the lesson!

"With pride, there are many curses. With humility, there come many blessings."
Ezra Taft Benson

138. In Limited Supply...

Penalty takers are in demand in every

business and workplace. However, supply is limited.

This season ensure you kick-off and succeed.......when the whistle blows!
Some people may say that you surely don't want, need or require a team of penalty takers!
Well, let us imagine that you have managed with the help of your side to get to the UEFA Champions League Cup Final. It is being held at the Bernabeu Stadium in Spain, in front of 85,000 fanatical supporters.
The enthralling game has finished after 90 minutes at two goals a piece. No further goals are scored in the 30 minutes of extra-time that followed.
Your players have done you proud. However your top striker was injured just after the hour mark and was replaced by a relatively inexperienced youngster, although he is without doubt going to be a quality player in the making. And although you held on for a draw in the final two minutes of extra-time, your designated penalty taker, who has scored 13 out of his 14 previous attempts this

season was sent off for a 2nd bookable offence!

As you look around the ten players who finished the match in the soaring Madrid heat in the middle of May, many with sweat dripping from their brow having given their all, others energy sapped from their bodies. It's decision time.....Which 5 exhausted players do you choose to take the vital spot kicks?

Let us assume that from the 5 penalties taken by the opposition and the 5 from yourselves, all are successful. So, so far no one has missed. All ten have been scored......it is still all level.

Now we move on to sudden death, one penalty kick apiece. Remember these will now be taken by the players who initially were omitted, did not want to be considered, were nervous, scared, overwhelmed at the thought. They would have exited the stadium rather than have this responsibility thrust upon them!!!

So are you still sure that you do not need A TEAM of penalty takers?

Of course you do!

We need individuals who will continually work on their character traits, those with a healthy desire to consistently develop and improve their talents, keen to work on their abilities, willing to learn from other more experienced team-mates. Strengths that will undoubtably enable them to be fantastic colleagues, valued team members that if and when they are required to step up to the spot.......will do so confidently, willingly and prove themselves to be remarkable penalty takers - whether they score or not!

139. When You Wish Upon a Star...

Who better to have a 'special wand' than the staff of Disney. In California it's called the Magic Kingdom after all. DisneyWorld is located in Florida, where they have the Orlando Magic basketball team, and at Disneyland Paris, the French language just makes everything sound beautiful and elegant, adding a touch of mystery, mystique and magic!

They talk about what they are empowered to do and share the experience with their guests, not customers.

We are often encouraged to think outside the box. Walt Disney asked, "what box?" He was a visionary. He believed that no box should exist in the first place. Everything was attainable and could be achieved. Dream big, aim high and watch the magic happen!

140. Drop Feathers...

If you want to teach a principle - Don't throw stones...drop feathers. It may be someone will pick one up, and think how beautiful it is!

I cannot attribute this wise statement to a specific author, but what a wonderfully simple, yet powerful concept to embrace.

141. Leadership...

Stephen R. Covey passed away in July 2012, leaving behind an unmatched legacy with his teachings about leadership, time management, effectiveness, success, and even love and family.

A multimillion-copy bestselling author of self-help and business classics, Dr. Covey strove to help readers recognise the key elements that would lead them to personal and professional effectiveness.

Let me share with you two short gems on Leadership from Dr. Covey's vast and memorable collection:

1. " You can buy a person's hand, but you can't buy his heart. His heart is where his enthusiasm, his loyalty is. You can buy his back, but you can't buy his brain. That's where his creativity is, his ingenuity, his resourcefulness."

2. "You can quickly grasp the important difference between leadership and management if you envision a group of producers cutting their way through the jungle with machetes. They're the producers, the problem solvers. They're cutting through the undergrowth, clearing it out.

The managers are behind them, sharpening their machetes, writing policy and procedure manuals, holding muscle development programs, bringing in improved technologies, and setting up working schedules and compensation programs for machete wielders.

The leader is the one who climbs the tallest tree, surveys the entire situation, and yells, 'Wrong jungle!'

But how do the busy, efficient producers and managers often respond? "Shut up! We're making progress."

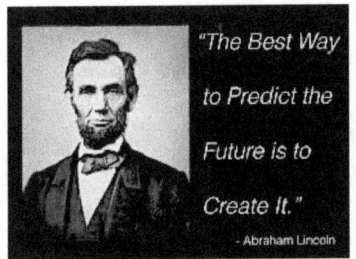

142. Create Your Own Future...

Make sure that everything you say and do from now on is consistent with the beliefs that you want to have and the person that you want to become. Over time, you will completely re-program yourself for success.

In more than three thousand studies of leaders conducted over the years, there is a special quality that stands out, one quality that all great leaders have in common. It is the quality of *vision*.

Leaders have vision. Non-leaders do not.

What is it that leaders think about most of the time? The answer is that *leaders think about the future* and where they are going and what they can do to get there. Nonleaders, on the other hand, think about the present and the pleasures and problems of the moment. They think and worry about the past and what has happened that cannot be changed.

 *This is one of the most important discoveries ever made. Just imagine! The further you think into the future, the better decisions you will make in the present to assure that that future becomes a reality.*

143. The Value of Charm...

"The most valuable commodity in the world isn't gold or diamonds - it's charm!"

Professional speaker Mark Sanborn commented on meeting President Bill Clinton: "He projected a totally 'in the moment' focus on each person he met. He exuded warmth, he seemed a man genuinely interested in liking you, and not concerned with whether or not you liked him. How much of that was genetic and how much developed I can only speculate. All I know is that I was, in that brief moment of meeting, totally charmed by a person I neither agreed with nor even expected to like."

Those who charm get great delight in giving others pleasure. They usually get listened to and often get extra chances. They are given opportunities that others may never get. They can be forgiven for things others would be lambasted or condemned for.

The deepest craving of human nature is the need to feel valued and valuable. The secret of charm is therefore simple: Make Others Feel Important!

Think of the most charming person you know. Observe the person's behaviour. Try to identify what he or she does when being charming. Watch the effect it has on others and use what you observe and learn as motivation to become, in your own way, just like your model - charming, persuasive and admirable!

144. Make Others Feel Significant...

There's a big difference between appreciating people and making them feel significant. Of course, you want to appreciate others. But even more than that, you need to make those important people in your life feel that they matter. Success - both personally and professionally - is hard to achieve without others who fill gaps for you and support you. There is rarely an exception to this. Think of people in your life. Who has really impacted your career and your family? Do you make those people feel as if they're irreplaceable? Do you brag on them in the presence of others? Do you give them credit for all they do for you? Do you ask for their opinions on things important to you and to the success of their company? Do you tell them how much you value their advice? Are you interested in the things they care about?

How about your family? Do you go the extra mile to make your spouse and children feel important to you? Do you listen to them, value their input, compliment them often and do special things for them?

People blossom when they feel loved. How can you do the same for the special people in your life?

145. Driven by Customer Service...

No matter who you are, what you do, where you work, or how much money you make, you can learn a lot from a cab driver - especially when it is Taxi Terry, a successful self-starting entrepreneur who combines passion with effort and skill to create distinction in his job and in his life.

Bestselling author and Hall of Fame speaker Scott McKain was so impressed by Terry's joyful approach to customer service, he incorporated the driver's inspiring personal philosophy and uplifting advice into his business speeches at corporate events - with stunning success.

These are the 7 Tenets of Taxi Terry:

1. Set high expectations - then, exceed them!
2. Delivering what helps the customer...helps you.
3. Customers are people - so, personalize the experience.
4. Think logically - then act creatively and consistently.
5. Make the customer the star of your show!
6. Help your customers to come back for more.
7. Creating joy for your customer will make your work - and life - more joyful!

*Feel inspired by the ideas and insight of Taxi Terry...and go create the best guide to **customer service** you will ever need.*

146. A Secret Cautionary Tale...

Californian Roy Raymond set up Victoria's Secret back in 1977. A Stanford business graduate, Raymond hit on the idea when he tried to buy some underwear for his wife and was left feeling like he was about to be put on some sort of register. What if there was a nice place that men could feel comfortable in; a shop where they could browse at their leisure without having to manically flash their wedding bands?

He opened his first store in Palo Alto, now famous for breeding 27-year-old trillionaires, but then just a sleepy California suburb. The shop was the quintessential American vision of an English boudoir. The brand was called Victoria's Secret after Queen Victoria - the figurehead of a notoriously repressed era.

Raymond launched a Victoria's Secret catalogue, which in pre-Internet days went down very well, and allowed the brand to reach customers across America. By 1982, he had opened another three stores in the Bay Area and the company was making more than $4m in annual sales.

And yet he was reportedly nearing bankruptcy. In marketing only to men, Raymond forgot the basic principle that most of a women's underwear drawer will be purchased by her and not her other half.

Alienating the main consumers of women's underwear, i.e. women, was probably not the most sensible idea, and in 1982, Raymond sold the company to sportswear mogul Leslie Wexner for around $1m.

Wexner's hunch paid off. By 1995 when the brand launched its now iconic catwalk shows, featuring supermodels including Helena Christiansen and Tyra Banks, Victoria's Secret had become a $1.9bn company, with 670 stores across the US.

Today the brand control a huge 35pc of America's lingerie market (according to Forbes), with sales over $6.6bn in 2013.

Sadly, despite his original foresight, Raymond did not share in this success. After staying on as president for a year, he left to form another retail and catalogue company, this time in children's clothes. His brand My Child's Destiny was declared bankrupt within two years, leaving Raymond personally liable for its debts. The Raymonds lost two homes and their cars. In 1993, after another failed business attempt – this time a children's bookshop – the couple divorced.

As far as Victoria's Secret went, Raymond's instinct was spot on, but his implementation lacked the understanding of his successor, leaving him to become a cautionary tale for entrepreneurs. In August 1993, Roy Raymond jumped to his death from San Francisco's Golden Gate Bridge.

147. With the Help of Others...

Jimmy Shand was one of Scotland's greatest musical ambassadors. He was 'the King of Scottish Dance Band Music' for over 50 years. Many years ago I read his autobiography. The book was not big enough to record all the people Jimmy had met, had made music with and received many kindnesses from over the years. Much of what Jimmy had achieved would not have been possible without the love, support and encouragement of his wife Anne, and his close and extended family. Having a solid foundation at home gave him the confidence to express his wonderful talent to millions of others.

Surround yourself with greatness, create an infrastructure of love and gratitude. Promote strong principles that allow you to relish each day and continue to make it a pleasure to go about your daily schedule with both purpose and focus.

148.Cycling to Success...

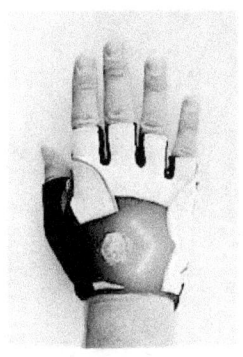

Why can't they just stay off the road! Drivers and cyclists may never live in peace, but Zackees Turn Signal Gloves can help toward repairing that strained relationship. By extending your arm, bright LED lights on the glove blink, alerting drivers and others around you that you're taking a right...or a left.

Created by a Google engineer, the gloves are made with high-quality textiles, making them both comfortable and washable - plus, they have a two month battery life.

For cyclists, those gloves just might save their lives. What amazing ground breaking idea, invention or service are you going to produce?

149. Rules Protect the Weak, but Limit the Strong...

 "Enough said!"

150. Be Persuasive...

There are certain words that dramatically increase persuasion and response. Here are some of them.

1. **You.** Aren't you more interested in you than me? All human beings are naturally self-interested. We want to know how we can survive, improve our well-being, get rich, solve problems, etc. The more you use the word "you" in your copy, the better it is for you.

As a rough guide "You's need to outnumber "I's" and "We's" by two or three to one.

2. **Free, At No Charge, At No Cost, Without Charge, Complimentary.** Doesn't everyone want something for free? Most people are naturally drawn to advertising offering something for FREE. I remember speaking to an advertising executive who told me, with frustration, how he would spend hours crafting an ad which would be beaten by something much simpler with the word "FREE" in the headline.

3. **New, Now.** In conversation people often talk about the latest thing. This is because people want to know what is new. You can often start a headline with "New." And even if your product isn't particularly new you can always substitute NOW. It implies newness and recency in the same way.

4. **Revealed, Exposed, Secret, Hidden, Uncovered, Discovered, Unveiled, Released, Revolutionary.** Everyone likes to know a secret...and your prospects are no exception. Tell them you're giving them

access to something very few people have...and they'll be hooked.

5. **Because.** We do things for a reason. And we want a reason for things. If you make a claim in your copy and say "because", then the reason will be accepted, whether it makes sense or not.

6. **Naturally, Easily, Effortlessly, Smoothly, Quietly, Readily.** No one wants something that entails a lot of work...all these words make it all seem so easy.

7. **Guarantee, Money-Back, Risk-Free.** The biggest barrier to business is trust. These words help build trust by removing the risk from the buyer and putting it on the shoulders of the seller.

8. **Unique, Exclusive, Limited, Special, Select, Elite, Matchless, Unrivalled, Unparalleled, Unmatched, Unequalled.** Your prospects want to think they're getting the best.

9. **Who, What, Which, When, How.** These are great standby words to create headlines when you are hard pushed to think of something. They are also a great way to plan out longer copy for something like a brochure or leaflet. Basically when you answer these questions you tell people what they want to know in a clear, concise way.

10. **Finally...avoid a lot of adjectives, especially unreal superlatives.** Haven't you read an awful lot of brochures which talk about the best XYZ or the very finest ABC? Everyone is telling you they are the best. Everyone simply cannot be the best, so consumers naturally tend to disbelieve you when you tell them that you are the best.

The words you use when you communicate to your customers (online or in letters, brochures, conversations, etc) will directly impact your Sales.

151. Two Paths...

The paragraphs below are an abridged version of a talk entitled "The Two Greatest Days in Your Life," by leadership expert John C. Maxwell. As a speaker and author Maxwell has written more than 60 books. Enjoy the article...

"Over the years, as I have watched and listened to successful leaders, I have discovered a common thread: They know why they're here. Knowing their purpose in life gives them stability. And when others around them start abandoning their causes and jumping ship when life gets tough, these people use this assurance to steady the boat, to ride out the storm, because they have a true North Star.

Someone once said there are two great days in our lives - the day we are born and the day we discover why.
Highly successful people have discovered why.

I think there are two paths you and I can take to help discover our purpose. The first is passion. What are you passionate about? What do you really care about? What would you live for; what would you die for?

Passion is not 100 percent foolproof, but it will get you into the location, the area, the neighbourhood of what your purpose really is. Passion is what I call the "great energiser." It's no secret that passionate people have a lot of energy. That's why, when you see successful people, they love what they're doing and doing what they love.

People who are highly successful love the journey as much as the destination. And even though they might not have yet arrived, they remain encouraged because they still have fuel in their tanks from their incredible passion.

While passion will get you into the location, it's only about 80 percent accurate. The other path you can take to discover your purpose is 100 percent accurate - I guarantee it.

This is your Strength Zone path. In other words, you've got to find the path where you can answer the following questions: What do I do well? What are my strengths? What is my gift? What is the talent that sets me apart from everybody else? Everyone has a "uniqueness" that would enable them to rise above the rest, if they just discover it, fine-tune it, work hard and grow in it.

Here is the best way to explain it. People simply will not pay for average. So why do so many of us think we can have an average business or an average career or an average life and make a difference? Average doesn't make a difference.

For more than thirty years I have been on a personal growth plan. Growth is not an automatic process. If you are going to grow, you need to do so intentionally."

Highly successful people know their purpose in life, grow to their maximum potential and sow seeds that benefit others. They don't live for themselves. They understand what significance is. Significance is adding value to others.

152. The Book...

Persuasion is something we *do* to people and influence is something that we *have*.

This book is not just about understanding how the process of influence works and making yourself happier, it's also about challenging yourself to establish what your goals are.

 *Life is a game and this book will help you improve the odds.*

153. When No One is Watching...

Perhaps the most important thing you do as a leader is to be a good role model. Lead by example. Walk the talk. Live the life. Always carry yourself as though everyone is watching, even when no one is watching.

Good leaders are completely reliable. People can take them at their word and trust that they will do what they say. They make promises carefully, and then always keep their word.

154. Engage...

To get customers interested in what you're selling, make your sales message about your customers.

You're excited about your company, right? You're proud of your products, right? Therefore, your best strategy, when talking to a customer, is to tell the story of your company and its products with excitement and enthusiasm, right?

Wrong!

Customers don't care about your company. They don't care about its products.
And they certainly don't care about your personal feelings towards your company and its products.

What customers care about is... themselves!

The failure to realize this simple fact about human nature is why most companies have sales and marketing messages that make customers shrug.

Over the past few years, I have reviewed hundreds of sales messages. In almost every case, these messages are all about the seller and the products being sold. They leave it up the customer's imagination to figure out "what does all of this mean to ME?"

Which leads us to the two sentences that are the most important to your customers and prospective customers:

1. "Our clients hire us to provide [benefit(s) to the client]"

2. "They hire us, rather than somebody else, because [something unique that the competition doesn't have but the customer values]"

Notice that both of these sentences position you, the seller, as a catalyst that helps the customer achieve the customer's goals, and then positions your firm as the only catalyst that can do the job right.

Here are some examples:

Example 1:

Wrong:

"Acme specializes in consumer-validated 360 degree product development via our patented sequential market research process, which has been successfully applied to the fast moving consumer goods industry. In the past 24 months we have created $2.9 billion in innovative business opportunities for our clients.

Right:

"Consumer goods companies hire Acme to create new products for them, and market both those new products and their existing products. Because we base our efforts on meticulous research into target markets, we've generated over $2.9 billion in new revenue for our clients over the past two years."

Example 2:

Wrong:

"Several years ago, Acme saw a problem in the transportation industry: that the process of valuing and transferring ownership of transportation businesses is a very unstable and unpredictable process. And as a result, many hardworking owners were unable to cash out of their businesses when they wanted to. Basically they shut the doors. Acme is built to specifically address this industry problem--we help buyers and sellers alike start a new chapter in life.

Right:

"Entrepreneurs hire Acme to sell or acquire transportation businesses like limousines, buses, and ambulances. We can help them negotiate the best and most reasonable price because we have 20 years of experience with this type of business."

Can you see the difference? The original messages force the customer to figure out what it all means to the customer.

The rewritten messages express what's being provided from the customer's viewpoint.

 *In other words, to engage customers in a conversation about the possibility of hiring you or your firm, make the message about the CUSTOMER rather than about YOU.*

155. Penalty Taker Questions...

People want to be sure that you both hear and understand them. They want to feel that you know what is really crucial to them. People like people who show a genuine desire to understand their situation, an unfeigned interest in what is the most important thing to them.

The following questions, all have one thing in common: they allow you to 'dig deeper,' giving you the information and the opportunity to influence.

1. 'I wonder if you could help me?'
2. 'What makes you say that?'
3. 'Can you tell me more about that?'
4. 'What can I do to help you?'
5. 'If you were me, what would you do?'
6. 'Why do you ask?'
7. 'How do you feel about that?'

Work on your exploration skills, continue to delve a little deeper and ask these **Magnificent Seven** *questions. You'll be amazed - the more you ask them, the closer you will find people are to you. They will confide in you, turn to you, rely on you and more fully trust you!*

Footnote:

I had the wonderful opportunity throughout May 2015 to work closely with four inspiring individuals, first rate Penalty Takers. I would go so far as to call them....... Super Heroes!

They know who they are, and I look forward to watching their progress in the coming years. The following is just a selection of madcap words, phrases, song titles and monikers we used around each other that helped us bond. We shared fun and laughter, numerous teaching experiences, spiritual moments, sporting opportunities and were involved in several service projects together. Each possessed their own wand and on many occasions, had the chance to create outstanding,  memorable, 'TADA!' moments.

So: Let me tell you a story; Bless your Beautiful Hide; Big Butt; Sean Connery; Good, Better, Best; Pros and Cons; Seven Brides for Seven Brothers; We are Livingston Ward; Volleyball; Ambrosia; Glaikit; Airdrie; Ukulele; Kiss the Girl; Tarzan and Jane; Above and Beyond; Care and Candor; Sittin' on the dock of the bay; P-day; The Viaduct Walk; Master of the House; Under the Sea; Honeycrunch, Babes, Peeps and Hen; Flogging Molly; Bright Golden Haze on the Meadow; Charm; Manamana; Cherry on Top; Big M; Little M; Dad; Las Vegas - Sodom and Gomorrah; Georgia on my mind; The Caves; Pa'erson; Two t's; The Word of the Day and finally - He was a Paratrooper you know!!!!!!!!

To: The Black Widow, Wonder Woman, Spiderman and Mr. Fantastic.... always remember the honour, the privilege and pleasure was all mine.

It's In Your Actions...

"If you learn just one strategy from this book that will attract better clients and increase your success, then the investment in your personal effectiveness will have paid for itself many times over."

 *Pass it on to others, share your wealth... and get the result you richly deserve!!!!*

THE END

...or is it just the beginning?

Smile It Confuses People!

About Me...

Michael Patterson - I love to work with individuals, leaders, teams and organisations to help them grasp their true potential, achieve goals and enhance performance.

Find out more about me, my work and how I may be able to help you or your organisation become Penalty Takers at www.timeforkickoff.com. or directly at -

michaeldavidpatterson121@gmail.com